Go[...]

[...] the

Equalizer

By Eric Mumford

P.O. Box 3709 ❖ Cookeville, TN 38502
931.520.3730 ❖ lc@lifechangers.org

PLUMBLINE

Published by:

LIFECHANGERS®
LIBRARY SERIES

P.O. Box 3709 | Cookeville, TN 38502
(800) 521-5676 | www.lifechangers.org

All Rights Reserved
ISBN 978-1-940054-12-4

God Magnified, Part 11
Encountering the Equalizer

Contents

Introduction: God Magnified 4

Setting Earth on the Pillar of Justice 8

Preserving Freedom and Coequality 18

The Equalizer 34

"Jesus called them to Himself" 44

Exposing 'Even-steven' 49

Jesus Out-socialists the Socialists 56

Judged Through a Man 68

Son Made Perfect Forever 71

Victim of Man's Injustice 76

Mirror of God's Glory 83

Introduction: God Magnified

God is an "**Us**" (Gen. 1:26, 3:22, 11:7; Isa. 6:8).

"God is **one**" (Deut. 6:4; Mark 12:29).

"God is **Agape**" (1John 4:8, 16).

"God is a **sun**" (Ps. 84:11).

"**Holy**, **Holy**, **Holy** is the Lord God, the **Almighty**" (Rev. 4:8; Isa. 6:8).

"God is **Light**" (1John 1:5).

"The eternal God is a **dwelling place**" (Deut. 33:27).

God is "**in Christ**" (Col. 2:9; 2 Cor. 5:19; Eph. 4:32).

"God is **Spirit**" (John 4:24).

"God is **true**" (John 3:33).

God is "**Most High**" (Ps. 57:2; Acts 7:48).

"The Lord is a God of **justice**" (Isa. 30:18).

"The Lord, whose name is *Jealous*, is a **jealous** God" (Ex. 34:14).

"God is a **consuming fire**" (Deut. 4:24; Heb. 12:29).

God is three **sacrificial Self-sharers**

God Magnified, Part 11
Encountering the Equalizer

By Eric Mumford

The "*God is*" statements of the Scriptures are like pillars of a covered porch built around the entire circumference of **the kingdom of God**; each pillar serves as a lens to see and understand the next: "God *is* a dwelling place." Progressive magnification of these "*God is*" declarations leads to a three-dimensional understanding of this eternal cohabitation and draws us to enter and participate as *self-sharers* through the God-Man Jesus in the "eternal life" of Father, Son, and Spirit. As emigrants to the kingdom, we are pioneering forward together into this unfolding revelation of **the fusion of the Trinity**.

In the previous volume, *God Magnified Part 10: Observing Coequality and Justice*, we began to examine the eleventh pillar, "**the Lord is a God of justice**" (Isa. 30:18), and discovered why justice and Agape (sacrificial self-sharing love) are one, inseparable reality rooted in the very nature our Triune-Creator as three Coequals. Sacrificial self-sharing constitutes "the law" of our Triune-God and the bedrock of true justice, which **preserves freedom and coequality** among all individuals who enter and participate together in the cohabitation of the kingdom that Father, Son, and Spirit have purposed to share with us. Lawfulness is Trinity-likeness.

We also learned that our misconceptions of the nature and justice of God, combined with the de-gene-rate, eros nature of "the father of the lie" (John 8:44) at work within us, also known as "the law of sin and death" (Rom. 8:2), compel us to "**accuse** [*lit. categorize*]" (Rev. 12:10) and judge one another in a manner that causes relational fission. Man-made justice in this world is always **reactionary** and counter-reactionary; therefore, it "comes out perverted" (Hab. 1:3-8). God's justice is always **proactive**—a redemptive manifestation of the very Presence of the Trinity among us, which exposes, confronts, and corrects our **lawlessness: incapacity to share**. The cohabitation of the kingdom is one shared estate comprised of the unlocked, open gardens of our individual lives, and the law of Agape ensure that each of us behaves in a proper, godly (Trinity-like) manner while we are 'in' one another's gardens!

We recognized that as corrupt human beings (individualists) you and I are like **porcupines** who instinctually stab and torment one another and have an innate aversion to sharing. To keep warm, a family of porcupines must huddle together in one, shared burrow, yet all of us must learn to do so very carefully! Justice is the gift of our Triune-God to keep us warm.

We defined five norms of **distributive justice**— equity, equality, invested authority, need, and responsibility—and found examples in the Scriptures of how the Spirit sovereignly applies these norms in each unique situation to preserve unity among us as coequal sharers of one, free, peaceful, fruit-bearing cohabitation.

Now, in this volume, *God Magnified: Encountering the Equalizer*, we will see how the Son of God was incarnated as the Man Jesus Christ in order that He might embody within Himself the Father and the Spirit—**three eternal Coequals**: "For in Him all the fullness of Deity dwells in bodily form…" (Col. 2:9). As the Nucleus of these three Coequals who abide in relational, inter-Personal fusion, Christ Jesus came as **the Equalizer** among corrupt, eros-driven human beings to embody and equitably distribute justice. See how encountering the Equalizer radically exposes our individualism; confronts self-worth-ship; revolutionizes our economy of values; and gives us new eyes to see the poor, our neighbors, our friends, and even our enemies as coequals:

> And there was a man called by the name of Zacchaeus; he was a **chief tax collector** and he was rich. Zacchaeus was trying to see who Jesus was, and was unable because of the crowd, for he was small in stature. So he ran on ahead and climbed up into a sycamore tree in order to see Him…. When Jesus came to the place, He looked up and said to him, "Zacchaeus, hurry and come down,

for today I must stay at your house." And he hurried and came down and **received Him** [*the Equalizer*] **gladly**…. Zacchaeus stopped and said to the Lord, "Behold, Lord, half of my possessions I will give to the poor, and if I have **defrauded** anyone of anything, I will **give back** four times as much [*e.g. distributive justice to my coequals*]." And Jesus said to him, "Today **salvation** [*the kingdom*] **has come to this house** [*cohabitation*]…" (Luke 19:2-9).

As a skilled opportunist, Zacchaeus distinguished himself in the economy of Worthless' world by buying and selling his own people for personal gain. However, encountering the Equalizer—"God in Christ"— not only brought the freedom, coequality, and justice of the kingdom into Zacchaeus as an individual but also among all those within his sphere of influence. As you and I encounter the Equalizer— "the Spirit of Christ" (Rom. 8:9)—and *receive Him gladly*, we are incorporated as coequal "members" of His own resurrected corpus, and we are acculturated into the kingdom of our Triune-God.

1. Setting Earth on the Pillar of Justice

The Scriptures specifically identify justice as one of the main, load-bearing "**pillars**" upon which the relational, inter-personal "infrastructure" of the kingdom of God rests. This series of *Plumblines* entitled *God Magnified* is certainly an inadequate representation of the full Reality of all that "*God is*"; nevertheless, in this limited model, **Pillar 12** is "the Lord is a God of justice" (Isa. 30:18). God spoke through David:

> When I select the appointed time, it is I [*three incorruptible Self-sharers*] who **judge with equity**; the earth and all [*corrupt individualists*] who dwell in it melt [*in the Presence of the fusion of the Trinity*]; it is I [*Holy, Holy, Holy*] who have **firmly set its pillars** [*freedom, coequality, and justice rest upon Who "God is"*]. I said to the **boastful**, "Do not boast [*in self-exaltation*]," and to the **wicked** [*self-indulgent opportunists*], "Do not lift up the horn [*of a conqueror*]; do not lift up the horn on high [*in upward descent*], do not speak with **insolent pride** [*Worthless' words: envious self-worth-ship*]" (Psa. 75:2-5).

Our Triune-Creator (the "Us" of our genesis) established the earth upon the load-bearing "pillar" of Their own freedom and coequality as sacrificial Self-sharers. However, human beings fell into self-worth-ship, de-gene-rated in corruption, matured as lawless opportunists, and multiplied injustice; therefore, "**the earth reels to and fro like a drunkard and it totters like a shack,** for its transgression is heavy upon it, and it will fall [*in upward descent*], never to rise again [*e.g. God has* *prepared a new creation*]" (Isa. 24:20). Individually and collectively, we all fell off "the pillar"!

The Patriarch Jacob was born a calculative opportunist, a "supplanter" (Gen. 27:36). In order to convert him into "Israel"—a sacrificial self-sharing man fit to steward the inheritance of God's promise to Abraham—the Spirit "enrolled" him in a 20-year life-lab of suffering in the service of a superior opportunist: his father-in-law, Laban.

> Laban replied to Jacob, "…So now come, let us make a covenant, you and I, and let it be a witness between you and me [*e.g. since it is impossible for us to trust one another*]." Then Jacob took **a stone** [*type of Christ the Cornerstone*] and set it up as **a pillar** [*of justice*].… So they took stones and made a heap…. Laban said, "This heap is a witness between you and me this day…. **May the Lord watch between you and me** when we are absent one from the other. If you mistreat my daughters, or if you take wives besides my daughters, although no man is with us, see, **God** [*Triune-Justice*] **is witness between you and me**.… This heap is a witness, and **the pillar is a witness**, that I will not pass by this heap to you for harm, and you will not pass by this heap and this pillar to me for harm. The God of Abraham…judge between us" (Gen. 31:43-53).

True justice cannot be found anywhere in Worthless' world because all of its inhabitants, both secular and religious, are corrupt. **Justice must come down from above** and be humbly received and embraced by repentant, self-emptied men:

> Therefore because you impose heavy rent on the poor and exact a tribute of grain from them [*e.g. practice opportunism*], though you have built houses of well-hewn stone, yet you will not live in them [*reaping futility from Worthless' world economy*].... Hate evil [*self-indulgence*], love good [*sacrificial self-sharing*] and establish justice [*freedom and coequality*] in the gate!... **Let justice roll down like waters** [*from the Triune-Most High*] **and righteousness** [*reciprocal gene-rosity*] **like an ever-flowing stream** [*e.g. re-gene-ration in the outpouring of the Spirit of Christ*] (Amos 5:11-24).

The source from which Father, Son, and Spirit implement justice in Their fallen creation is Their own coequality as sacrificial Self-sharers: "The **works** of God's hands are **truth** [*relational altruism*] and **justice** [*promoting and preserving relational coequality*]; **all His precepts are sure** [*incorruptible, unshakable*]" (Ps. 111:7). Father, Son, and Spirit now *work* together to re-gene-rate you and me in Their *own* sacrificial Self-sharing nature, to **mentor** us as sons and daughters in reciprocal gene-rosity, and

acculturate us into Their *own* cohabitation: "For **we are His workmanship**, created in Christ Jesus [*the Prototype Self-sharing Man*] for good works, which God prepared beforehand so that we would walk in them [*e.g. embodying and implementing true, kingdom justice in the earth*]" (Eph. 2:10). Paul revealed God's plan to incorporate us into "the pillar" of justice:

> I write so that you will know [*Triune-Justice:*] **how one ought to conduct himself in the household of God** [*cohabitation of sacrificial self-sharers in fusion*] which is **the church** [*many-membered body/corpus*] **of the living God** [*three Self-sharers 'alive' to One Another and to us in Christ*], **the pillar and support of the truth** [*embodying and manifesting Triune-Agape as coequals in a world of corruption and injustice*] (1 Tim. 3:15).

Mankind has fallen off "the pillar," but Father, Son, and Spirit have purposed to reintroduce justice in the earth by **incorporating** you and me into the strength and solidarity of Their own load-bearing "pillar" so the lost inhabitants of the earth may come to "rest" upon us who are the many-membered corpus of the God-Man Jesus Christ!

God loves righteousness [*Agape: reciprocal gene-rosity*] **and justice** [*freedom and coequality among individual self-sharers*]; **the earth** [*reeling* *and tottering under the weight of injustice*] **is full of the lovingkindness** [*Agape: the law*] **of the Lord** [*manifested in and through us, the many-membered corpus of Christ*] (Ps. 33:5).

God's ultimate purpose is to "make all things new" (Rev. 21:5), but first God must reestablish His own people, you and me, on "the pillar" of justice: "For the anxious longing of the creation [*enslaved to corruption*] waits eagerly for the revealing of the sons of God.... For those whom He foreknew, He also predestined to become **conformed** [*lit. morphed*] **to the image of His Son** [*the Prototype sacrificial Self-sharing Man*], so that He would be the **firstborn among many** [*gen-uine, coequal, incorruptible*] **brethren** (Rom. 8:19, 29).

God's ultimate plan to set the earth on the pillar of justice is the **Son Jesus**, but in the time of the Old Testament judges, a sovereign, prophetic "**rehearsal**" took place through Hannah and her **son Samuel**. Hannah was deeply oppressed and afflicted because she was barren while "her rival," her husband's second wife, bore him children and "provoked Hannah bitterly to irritate her [*e.g. categorizing her as barren*]" (1 Sam. 1:6). Yet, by faith, Hannah received a promise from the Lord that she would bear a son. After the Lord opened her womb and she gave birth to Samuel, Hannah sacrificially shared her firstborn son with the Lord in **reciprocal gene-rosity**.

Hannah took her newly-weaned boy on the long

journey to the tabernacle in Shiloh and surrendered him to live there permanently, to be raised by the priests and fathered and mentored by the Triune-God of Agape. In a very dark period of Israel's history, when "**every man did what was right in his own eyes** [*lawlessness*]" (Judg. 17:6), Hannah dedicated Samuel to serve as a priest, a judge, and a prophet through whom God would reestablish the wayward, tottering people of Israel on "**the pillar**" **of justice**. Though Hannah could only visit Samuel once a year at the annual sacrifice, she carried this son in her heart day and night. As she participated in the **sacrificial Son-sharing Love** of the Trinity—a mother's comprehensive and continuous act of true worth-ship to God—Hannah voiced this prophetic song of the Spirit:

> There is **no one** [*individual created being*] **holy** [*eros-free, incorruptible*] **like the Lord** [*three sacrificial Self-sharers in perpetual fusion*]…nor is there any **rock** like our God [*unshakable Triune-Solidarity*]. Boast no more so very proudly [*as an individualist in upward descent*], do not let arrogance [*self-worth-ship*] come out of your mouth; for **the Lord is a God of knowledge**, and with Him **actions** [*and motives*] **are weighed** [*in the "balances" of Triune-Justice*]. The bows of the **mighty** [*predatory opportunists*] are shattered, but the **feeble** gird on strength ["*power is perfected in*

weakness"]. Those who were **full** [*self-indulged*] hire themselves out for bread, but those who were **hungry** [*self-emptied*] cease to hunger.... the Lord kills and makes alive; He **brings down** to Sheol and **raises up**. The Lord makes **poor** and **rich**; He brings **low**, He also **exalts**.

He [*God Most High*] raises the **poor** from the dust, He lifts the **needy** from the ash heap to make them sit with **nobles**, and inherit a seat of honor [*the way of downward ascent*]; for **the pillars of the earth are the Lord's** [*true justice and coequality rest upon all the Triune-God "is"*], and He set the world on them [*legal precedent: eternal Three-in-Oneness*]. He keeps the feet of His **godly ones** [*Trinity-like self-sharers*], but the **wicked** [*individualists*] are silenced in darkness [*eclipse*]; for not by might [*self-will/effort*] shall a man prevail. Those who **contend** with the Lord [*All-Three-Mighty*] will be **shattered** [*on Christ the Cornerstone; see Luke 20:18*]; against them He will thunder in the heavens, the Lord will **judge** the ends of the earth [*"God will judge the world in righteousness through a Man" Acts 17:31*]... (1 Sam. 2:1-10).

Hannah gave birth to Samuel, but she sacrificially shared him with God so he could be raised and fathered by Triune-Agape and **mentored** as an incorruptible steward-son. Learning to abide by the law of Agape and walk in God's justice are mentoring processes: "He has told you, O man, what is good; **and** what does the Lord [*Triune-Agape*] require of you but to **do justice** [*preserve freedom and coequality by sacrificial self-sharing*], to **love kindness** [*practice bearing and forbearing one another*], and to **walk humbly with your God** [*abide in fusion as a self-emptied self-sharing son/daughter*]?" (Micah 6:8). Samuel addressed the people of Israel:

> "I am old and gray…. I have walked before you from my youth even to this day. Here I am; bear witness against me before the Lord and His anointed. Whose ox have I **taken**, or whose donkey have I **taken**, or whom have I **defrauded?** Whom have I **oppressed**, or from whose hand have I taken a **bribe** to blind my eyes with it? I will restore it to you." They said, **"You have not defrauded us or oppressed us or taken anything from any man's hand."** He said to them, "The Lord is witness against you…that you have found nothing in my hand." And they said, "He is witness" (1 Sam. 12:2-5).

God worked through Samuel, a begotten son, to reestablish Israel upon "the pillar" of justice. Being fathered and mentored by Triune-Agape, **the son Samuel** became an imperfect, yet true type of Jesus,

God's "only begotten Son" (John 1:14; 3:16; 1 John 4:9)—a Man tested as a sacrificial Self-sharer, proven incorruptible, and perfected as God's 'Equalizer' among men:

When the fullness of time came, **God sent forth His Son**, **born of a woman**, **born under the Law** [*Moses' external Law*], so that He might **redeem** those [*lawless opportunists*] who were under the Law [*self-condemned*], that we might receive the **adoption as sons** [*re-gene-rated and mentored as self-sharers; the law of Agape written into our DNA*] (Gal. 4:4).

The "pillar" of justice upon which our Triune-God desires to establish the earth is literally you and me *gen-uinely* incorporated into the corpus of the God-Man Jesus. Individuals who cohabit with one another in Christ as Trinity-like self-sharers **embody and uphold the eternal Reality of Triune-Agape**— the truth, light, economy, and law of the kingdom of God—**amongst corrupt individualists** who are moving with the false-father in upward descent as captives of the deception, darkness, lawlessness, and **unreality** of Worthless' world.

Wash yourselves, make yourselves clean [*assimilate the incorruptible bloodline/DNA of Christ*]; remove the evil of your deeds [*self-indulgence motivated by self-worth-ship*] from

My sight. **Cease to do evil, learn to do good** [*practice sacrificial self-sharing*]; **seek justice** [*jealously advocate the freedom and coequality of others*], **reprove the ruthless** [*predatory opportunists*], defend the orphan, plead for the widow [*bear up the weak*] (Isa. 1:16-17).

2. Preserving Freedom and Coequality

It was for **freedom** that Christ set us free [*set free from self-worth-ship so I may freely participate as a sacrificial self-sharer in His kingdom*]; therefore keep standing firm [*abiding together as coequals in fusion in the God-Man Nucleus*] and do not be subject again to a **yoke of slavery** [*corruption in individualism*] (Gal. 5:1).

The "dwelling place" of the eternal kingdom, which Father, Son, and Spirit *are* and established within the God-Man Jesus to share with us, is a cohabitation of *free*, self-sharing individuals who are governed by **the internal law of Agape** and practice reciprocal gene-rosity together. It would not be possible for Father, Son, and Spirit to re-gene-rate, mentor, discipline, and mature us as sons and daughters in Their own image and likeness, and **acculturate** us into Their "dwelling place," unless They had *already* adopted us and brought us home to Themselves in Christ: "Beloved, now we are children of God, and it has not appeared as yet what we will be [*e.g. we are not yet fully re-gene-rated; we are still corruptible*]" (1 John 3:2).

In the magnetism of Agape, it is a joy for Father, Son, and Spirit to share Their own sacred cohabitation with us, but at the same time it is also a sustained sacrifice of longsuffering because we are **half-formed children** in whom "the law of sin and death" (Rom. 8:2) still operates. James referred to this old nature that persists in true believers as "all that **remains** of wickedness" (Jas. 1:21). Isn't it painfully obvious that you and I have not yet learned how to share, and we are constantly **misbehaving** in Father's House by mistreating, "accusing [*categorizing*]," exploiting, and disowning one another? Consequently, do we not **shame the Name** that our Triune-God has sacrificially shared with us? Not only did David himself misbehave and inflict injury on others in God's house, he also suffered untold agony from the corrupt behavior of his brothers:

> For it is not an **enemy** who reproaches me, then I could bear it, nor is it one who hates me who has **exalted himself against me** [*devalued and disowned me in self-worth-ship*], then I could hide myself from him. But it is you, a man, **my equal** [*lit. according to my valuation, worth*], my **companion** [*coequal*] and my familiar **friend**; we who had **sweet fellowship**

together [*e.g. reciprocal self-sharing*] **and walked in the house of God** [*e.g. sons adopted by three Self-sharers and mentored as brothers*]…. He has put forth his hands [*as an opportunist*] against those who were at **peace** with him; he has **violated** his covenant [*fusion agreement— the law of Agape*]…his heart was **war** [*fission, self-exaltation*] (Ps. 55:12-14, 20-21).

The cohabitation of the kingdom is vulnerable because Father, Son, and Spirit have sacrificially opened Their own sacred nest of rest to mankind and brought Their corruptible, half-formed children into it. Perhaps this sheds light on Jesus observation, "the kingdom of heaven **suffers violence** [*lit. is forcibly entered*] and violent men [*i.e. religious opportunists*] take it by force [*lit. seize it for themselves*]" (Matt. 11:12). In this cohabitation, **justice is God's means of keeping each individual free** from the tyranny of self-worth-ship, self-will, and self-indulgence still at work within *him*, and of **keeping all of us free** from the opportunism, oppression, and usury of others.

> **For you were called to freedom** [*free participation in the bountiful economy of the kingdom: reciprocal gene-rosity*], **brethren** [*Jesus' half-formed brothers and sisters*]; **only do not turn your freedom** [*cohabiting with 'givers' in the corpus of Christ*] **into an opportunity for the flesh** [*self-indulgent*

opportunism], but through Agape [*sacrificial self-sharing*] serve one another [*deny yourself and seek every opportunity to bear, forbear, and add to one another as coequals*] (Gal. 5:13).

In the following three paragraphs, Jürgen Moltmann shares the profound insight he received into the relational freedom and coequality of Father, Son, and Spirit, as well as the sacrifices They continually embrace to make us sharers in it:

The person who is truly **free** [*from self-worth-ship*] no longer has to choose [*to sacrificially share himself with others*]...the person who chooses has **the torment of choice** [*deny self or indulge self?*]. Anyone who has to choose is constantly threatened by **evil** [*temptation, corruption, opportunism*], by the **enemy** [*"the father of the lie"*], by **injustice** [*selfish gain at another's expense*], because these things are always present as **potentialities** [*opportunities in Worthless' world*]. **True freedom** is not the 'torment of choice,' with its doubts and threats; it is simply **undivided joy in the good** [*cherishing relational oneness at any personal cost; I will not disown and sell you*].... Love is a self-evident, unquestionable 'overflowing of goodness' [*from within: gene-rous DNA*] which is therefore never open to **choice** at any time....

God [*three coequal Self-sharers*] **is the One who loves in freedom**…. Freedom does not mean **lordship** [*i.e. Monarch, Proprietor, or capricious Judge*]; it means **friendship** [*reciprocal self-sharing*]. This freedom consists of **the mutual and common participation in life** [*one shared life: relational fusion*], and a communication in which there is **neither lordship nor servitude** [*self-sharing coequality*]. In their **reciprocal participation in life**, people become free beyond the limitation of their own individuality [*freedom to be sharers in the Oneness of the Triune-God*]. The triune God reveals Himself as love in the **fellowship** [*Self-sharing*] of the Father, the Son and the Holy Spirit. His freedom therefore lies in the *friendship* which He offers [*shares with*] men and women, and through which He makes them His friends.

God's freedom is His vulnerable love, His openness, the encountering kindness through which He **suffers** with the human beings He loves and becomes their **advocate** [*God in Christ*], thereby throwing open their future to them. God demonstrates His eternal freedom through His suffering and His sacrifice, through His self-giving and His patience. Through His freedom He keeps man, His image, and His world, creation, free—**keeps**

them free and pays the price for their freedom [*fulfilling His own law*]. Through His freedom **God waits** [*in longsuffering*] **for man's love**, for his compassion [*reciprocal gene-rosity*].... Through His freedom He does not only speak as Lord, but listens to us as a Father (Jürgen Moltmann, *The Trinity and the Kingdom*, p. 56-57).

The *internal* nature of Agape is a dynamic, living stimulus that is manifested through **spontaneity and risk**; no *external* set of laws or other form of *external* coercion can *make* me risk sacrificially sharing myself with another in a spontaneous way. Dynamic expressions of extraverted love issue forth from the "seed" of Christ's nature *within* me and spontaneously move me to risk in vulnerable, costly acts of gene-rosity toward God and others. The greater my *freedom* from corruption in self-worth-ship, the more Agape is *freely* and *spontaneously* expressed through me toward others.

Unless Father, Son, and Spirit afforded us sustained exposure to Themselves (allowing us to be near to Them) by sacrificially receiving us as eros-infected children into Their own house (incorporating us into the corpus of Christ), we could never "be made perfect [*lit. telios, mature*]" (Heb. 11:40), we could never be "**set free from slavery to corruption** [*mutual exploitation*] **into the freedom of the glory of the children of God**

[*the fusion oneness of mature, Trinity-like self-sharers*]"
(Rom. 8:21). Even now, as we are being re-gene-
rated, mentored, disciplined, acculturated, and
matured by practice, **justice** preserves the freedom
and coequality of each of us half-formed children
who cohabit together in Christ and holds us together
as one family, one body, especially in those times
when you and I willfully work against it!

In the kingdom of our Triune-God, the value
of each "member" as well as the value of the whole
"body" are cherished and continue appreciating.
*"**All for one and one for all**"* did not originate with
The Three Musketeers. It is the eternal, relational
dynamic of Father, Son, and Spirit, which the early
church called **perichoresis**: mutual indwelling and
interpenetration without loss of personal identity.
Relational fusion and inter-personal oneness
(Trinity-likeness John 17:22) cannot be achieved or
maintained without *preserving* individual freedom
so each of us is *free* to volutarily and perpetually
"lose his life" into Christ and share one life in one
cohabitation together in Him. Among half-formed
children who remain eros-infected, **justice is God's
means of preserving individual freedom and
relational coequality** so that each and all of us are
free to practice sacrificially sharing ourselves with one
another.

"**Correct me** [*the recovering individualist*], O
Lord, but **with justice** [*conforming me to Your law
of sacrificial self-sharing coequality*]; not with Your

anger [*e.g. teach me to yield self-will so Your severity is not necessary*]..." (Jer. 10:24). As a half-formed son, it is still a major difficulty for me to awaken from my self-absorbed condition and truly recognize and willingly acknowledge that **my selfish choices trespass upon and violate the freedom and coequality of all those around me**. I am a wayward son who seriously needs mentoring and discipline! According to the dynamic law of Agape, true justice is designed to redeem, correct, and discipline me:

> It is for **discipline** that you endure [*embracing God's law: sharing the daily cross*]; **God deals with you as with sons**; for what son is there whom his father does not discipline? But if you are without discipline, of which all have become partakers, then you are **illegitimate children** [*de-gene-rate orphans, 'takers'*] and not sons [*sharers of God's fuse-able DNA*].... but **Father disciplines us** [*interrupts self-indulgence, self-will, self-worth-ship*] for our good, so that we may **share His holiness** [*eros-free, fuse-able nature*] (Heb. 12:8-10).

The **freedom** that individuals experience in the kingdom can be described as "**influence without control**"—Father does not *force* you to share, and even when you stubbornly refuse to share, the law of Agape moves the other "members of the body" to sacrificially forbear and uphold you! The only force of control is *internal*—the "seed" of Christ's fuse-able nature within each individual and the indwelling Spirit of Christ Who nourishes and cultivates that seed: "the Agape of Christ controls us" (2 Cor. 5:14).

The Triune-God, "through His Spirit who dwells in you" (Rom. 8:11), writes the law of Agape into your DNA, mentors you as a sacrificial self-sharer, and disciplines you in justice. "For **the flesh** [*corrupt, eros nature*] sets its desire against the Spirit, and **the Spirit** [*the Re-gene-rator*] against the flesh; for these are in opposition to one another, so that you [*the half-formed son, a recovering eros-addict*] **may not do the things that you please** [*indulge 'me now' at the expense of another*]" (Gal. 5:17). Your part in this work of re-gene-ration is essentially **yielding to the Spirit**. From within, the Spirit invites you to deny and empty yourself; He moves you to embrace Father's discipline from a willing spirit and prompts you to intentionally practice reciprocal self-sharing with the other coequal members of Christ's body.

Eros is introverted love, self-love; *Agape* is extroverted love, self-sharing love. **Extroversion** is essential to our freedom from self-centeredness, so we may freely share ourselves. The youngest child in a family who constantly makes demands and whines in attention-seeking is "**dethroned**" when God adds a new baby to the family—another with whom the child now must **share** and even help to serve. As an immature believer, God mercifully provides opportunities to turn my focus outside of myself by entrusting others into my care whom I must learn to love in place of myself. John observed, "We know that we have passed out of **death** [*individualism, fission*] into **life** [*relational fusion*] because **we Agape the brothers** [*preserve the freedom and coequality of others by sacrificial self-sharing*]. He who does not Agape abides in death [*eros implosion*]" (1 John 3:14).

The justice of our Triune-God not only preserves individual and corporate freedom, justice also cultivates and preserves individual and relational **coequality**. Moses testified:

> **The awesome God** [*three, incorruptible Coequals fused as "one" by reciprocal Self-sharing*] **who does not show partiality**, nor takes a bribe. He **executes justice** for the **orphan** and the **widow**, and shows His love [*bountiful gene-rosity*] for the **alien** [*Gentile*] by giving him food and clothing. So show your love [*self-sharing gene-rosity*] for the alien, for **you were aliens** [*oppressed, exploited slaves*] in the land of Egypt (Deut. 10:17-19).

Paul affirmed, "**there is no partiality** [*lit. face; e.g. promoting a recognizable face above an unknown face*] **with God** [*three incorruptible Self-sharers*]" (Rom. 2:11). In other words, God is not **loyal**, "God is **faithful**" (1 Cor. 1:9). Unlike corrupt, calculative men who categorize one another, God never sides *with* man "A" (who is at fault) *against* man "B" (who is blameless) simply because He recognizes and knows the face of man "A". Loyalty can be bought; faithfulness cannot be bought. To gain an advantage over others in any arena of Worthless' world, we have learned "***It is who you know.***" In the crab-bucket of the secular and religious world, the individual whose face I recognize and who recognizes me will give me the edge I need. Paul clarified, "For he who does wrong [*devalues and exploits another*] will receive the consequences of the wrong which he has done, and that **without partiality** [*lit. face*]" (Col. 3:25). Consider how racial, national, tribal, socio-economic, and denominational 'face-recognition' multiplies injustice!

Before Jesus converted Saul into Paul, he had been deeply acculturated into the hierarchical social system of the Pharisees that operated according to the pretentions of rank, reputation, and partiality, but he was radically re-acculturated in the kingdom:

> But from those who were of **high reputation** [*lit. seemed to be something; e.g. the apostles*] (what they were makes no difference to me; God shows **no partiality**)—well those who were of reputation contributed nothing to me [*I received my call and authority directly from Christ*]. But on the contrary, seeing that I had been entrusted with the gospel to the uncircumcised, just as Peter had been to the circumcised (for He who effectually worked

for Peter in his apostleship to the circumcised effectually worked for me also to the Gentiles), and recognizing the grace that had been given to me, James and Cephas [*Peter*] and John, who were reputed to be pillars, **gave to me and Barnabas the right hand of fellowship** [*received us as coequals*]....

But when Cephas came to Antioch, **I opposed him to his face, because he stood condemned**. For prior to the coming of certain men from James, he used to eat with the Gentiles [*as coequals*]; but when they came, he began to withdraw and hold himself aloof, fearing the party of the circumcision. The rest of the Jews **joined him in hypocrisy** [*con-fusion*], with the result that even Barnabas was carried away by their hypocrisy. But when I saw that they were **not straightforward about the truth of the gospel** [*three Coequals revealed in Christ*], I said to Cephas in the presence of all, "If you, being a Jew, live like the Gentiles and not like the Jews, how is it that you compel the Gentiles to live like Jews?" (Gal. 2:6-9).

Mentored by the Spirit of Christ as a self-sharing brother among coequals, Paul instructed us:

Do not receive an **accusation** [*lit. katēgoros*] **against an elder** except on the basis of two or three witnesses. Those who continue in sin, rebuke in the presence of all, so that the rest also will be fearful of sinning…maintain these principles **without bias** [*lit. premature, corrupt judgment*], **doing nothing in a spirit of partiality** [*promoting the familiar face; overlooking the self-indulgence of reputable leaders*] (1 Tim. 5:19-21).

T. Austin Sparks received profound insight into the fission dynamic of partiality from this seemingly obscure verse: "Under the custody and charge of the sons of Merari shall be the boards of the tabernacle and the bars" (Num. 3:36).

I am glad the bars are mentioned as well as the boards. The bars are the things that **unite the whole**, and if those things are kept always under your eye you will not move in cliques and you will not have personal preferences, and ones and twos moving off on their own because they get on together. We have to remember that **in the body of Christ there is nothing clannish**, nothing that is merely of **human preference**, but all the members are held together in oneness [*relational, interpersonal fusion*]. That is a responsibility [*our daily work: reciprocal sacrificial self-sharing in coequality*]. How much damage [*fission*] has been done by preferences, by **human affinities** [*partiality: magnetism to those who think like* *'me'*] having a place among the Lord's people! There must be personal care, there must be a watching over the bars, all maintained together; "…being diligent to preserve the unity of the Spirit in the bond of peace" (Eph. 4:3).

We shall never keep the unity of the Spirit by **taking sides with one against another**. We may think that is care for the one. Oh, but what about the other [*coequal*]? **The bars will be corrective** [*instruments of justice*], will keep the **balance** [*i.e. left and right brains*], and will **give due regard to every member** [*preserve freedom and coequality*]. There must be **mutuality** in this responsibility, each one carrying his own weight before the Lord, and yet all one. Draw in your mind's eye **three squares**, **separate**, **standing each alone**, and you will have what represents a very great deal of the work for the Lord in our day [*anti-Christ*]…'You have your work, you have your particular line, I have mine! You go on with yours, and I will get on with mine, and don't let us get overlapping!'…The result is always loss [*fission, futility, famine*] (Sparks, *The Church of the Firstborn*, chap. 5).

Our mobile medical clinics which enter the slums, refugee camps, and impoverished regions of

Uganda illustrate God's mobile tabernacle. Teams of about 30 persons, including doctors, nurses, and non-medical staff who work together, are themselves a dwelling place—an 'outpost' of the kingdom—into which thousands are received one at a time and touched and treated in their body, soul, and spirit. Our Lord Jesus is only able to engage these multitudes through us, His many-membered body, when the law of Agape functions among us as a team of coequals. As one new Man, Christ is only able to touch this world with **mobility**, **agility**, and **dexterity** as we "grow up in all aspects into Him who is the head, even Christ, from whom the whole body, being fitted and held together by what every joint supplies, according to the proper working of each individual part…" (Eph. 4:15-16).

The blueprints of the relational, inter-personal infrastructure into which we have been invited to cohabit in Christ come directly from the "Us" of our genesis. The law of Father, Son, and Spirit is profoundly **inclusive**, and the justice of our "incorruptible" Triune-God preserves the freedom and **coequality** of all:

> Thus says the Lord, "**Preserve justice** [*individual freedom and relational coequality*] **and do righteousness** [*practice sacrificial self-sharing*], for My salvation is about to come and My righteousness to be revealed [*"God in Christ": the Equalizer*]. How blessed is the

man who does this [*embraces and practices the law of Triune-Agape*], and the son of [*de-gene-rate*] man who takes hold of it [*receives the re-gene-rative seed of Christ*].... Let not the **foreigner** who has joined [*fused*] himself to the Lord say, 'The Lord will surely separate me [*in fission*] from His people [*e.g. act inequitably*].' Let not the **eunuch** say, 'Behold, I am a dry [*fruitless*] tree.'" For thus says the Lord, "To the eunuchs who...**choose what pleases Me** [*"seek first His"*], and hold fast My covenant [*reciprocate Triune-Agape*], to them I will give in My house [*cohabitation*] and within My walls a memorial, and **a name better than that of sons and daughters**; I will give them an **everlasting name** [*Our one shared name*] which will not be cut off.

"Also the **foreigners** who join [*fuse*] themselves to the Lord, to minister to Him, and to love the name of the Lord [*in place of making a name for themselves*], to be His [*self-emptied*] servants, every one who...holds fast My covenant; even those **I will bring to My holy** [*eros-free*] **mountain** and make them joyful in My house of prayer [*cohabitation of coequal burden-bearers*].... For **My house** [*Jesus: the God-Man Nucleus*] will be called **a house of prayer for all the peoples** [*"every tribe, tongue, people and nation" in coequality*]." The

Lord God, who gathers the dispersed of Israel, declares, "Yet others [*Gentiles*] I will gather to them [*incorporate into the corpus of Christ*], to those already gathered" (Isa. 56:1-8).

3. The Equalizer

The prophet Isaiah foretold how the God of **justice** would enter Worthless' corrupt, hierarchical world of **injustice** and engage its captives Man to man in and through Christ Jesus—*The Equalizer*:

Justice is turned back, and righteousness stands far away; for **truth** has stumbled in the street [*we have fallen off the pillar of justice*], and **uprightness cannot enter** [*our impenetrable fortress of self-worth-ship*]. Yes truth [*relational altruism*] is lacking; and he who turns himself aside from evil [*refuses to be con-fused with other opportunists*] makes himself a prey [*i.e. kill or be killed*].

Now the Lord saw and it was **displeasing** in His sight that there was **no justice** [*coequality*]. And He saw that there was **no** [*gene-rous*] **man**, and was astonished that there was no one to intercede [*seek first the interests of others*]; then **His own arm** [*Son of the Triune-God—"the arm of the Lord revealed" Isa. 53:1*] **brought salvation to Him**, and **His righteousness** [*extreme Self-forsaking Love*] **upheld Him**. He [*God in Christ*] put on righteousness like a breastplate, and a helmet of salvation on His head; and He put on garments of vengeance for clothing and wrapped Himself with **zeal** [*jealous-for love*] as a mantle (Isa. 59:14-17).

Consider the profound humility of Father, Son, and Spirit Who are so **bound** to corrupt, wayward human beings in sacrificial Self-sharing love, **They consider *Themselves* in need of "salvation."** God Most High (three Coequals who exalt One Another) needed a Man of justice to *uphold* Them among *fallen* mankind! While Jesus, the Nucleus of the Triune-God, was in Mary's womb, this young virgin spoke forth '***The Magnificat***'. Father and Spirit were indwelling "the Child" Who was forming within Mary, a girl who comprehensively shared herself: body, soul, and spirit. The few, choice words that the Spirit chose to speak forth *through* Mary revealed **the coming of God's 'Equalizer' among men**:

My **soul** exalts the Lord, and my **spirit** has rejoiced in God my Savior. For He has regard for the humble state of His bondslave [*my **body** is His temple*]; for behold, from this time on all generations will count me blessed [*one invited to share in the life of three sacrificial Self-sharers*]. For the **Mighty One** [*All-Three-Mighty*] has done great things for me; and

Holy is His name [*"Holy, Holy, Holy" share one Nucleus and name: "Jesus, the Holy One of God"*]. And His mercy is upon generation after generation toward those who fear Him.

He has done mighty deeds with **His arm** [*the Son: "the arm of the Lord revealed"*]; He has **scattered those who were proud** in the thought of their heart [*self-worth-ship, self-exaltation*]. He has brought down rulers from their thrones [*upward descent*], and has **exalted those who were humble** [*downward ascent*]. He has filled the **hungry** with good things [*Jesus' flesh: three "Ingredients" in one Cake*]; and sent the **rich** [*self-indulgent*] away empty-handed... (Luke 1:48-53).

God appointed John the Baptist to serve as a "forerunner" to Christ, to plow up the rocky soil of corrupt human hearts in preparation for the coming of the Equalizer Who, as a Man, would embody Triune-Justice amidst the captives of Worthless' world:

The voice of one crying in the wilderness [*a wasteland of injustice, oppression, famine*], "Make ready the way of the Lord [*the incarnate Son of Triune-Agape*], make His paths **straight** [*Light will pierce mankind's eclipse, flooding de-gene-rate hearts and minds*], every ravine will be **filled**, and every mountain and hill will be **brought low** [*lit. leveled; e.g. restoring coequality*]; the **crooked** will become **straight** [*eros "hooks" hammered out into "arrows" of unconditional Agape*], and the **rough roads smooth**; and all [*corrupt, de-gene-rate*] flesh will see the salvation of God [*Jesus: Antidote for the living dead*]" (Luke 3:4-6).

The Antidote, which the Triune-God sacrificially provided and continues to prescribe, is the Nucleus of Their own Self-sharing Life: **a King Who washes feet**, Who impoverishes Himself to make others rich, Who "lays down His life for the sheep" (John 10:11), and Who "did not come to be served, but to serve, and to give His life a ransom for many" (Matt. 20:20-28). This path made straight through Worthless' corrupt, hierarchical world is the sacrificial Self-sharing way of Father, Son, and Spirit—"I AM WHO I AM" (Ex. 3:14)—**embodied** in the Person of Christ: "I AM the way and the truth and the life" (John 14:6).

When Zacchaeus encountered the Equalizer, "he received Him gladly...and said, 'Behold, Lord, half of my possessions I will give to the poor [*as my coequals*], and if I have defrauded anyone of anything, I will give back four times as much'" (Luke 19:6-8). This way of relational freedom, coequality, justice, and peace is only attainable to those who recognize, receive, and reciprocate the sacrificial

Self-sharing Love of the Triune-God in Christ and practice it together as "lambs" who follow Him:

> The eyes of the proud [*captives of self-worship*] also will be abased [*upward descent*]. But **the Lord of hosts** [*three humble, inclusive Self-sharers*] will be **exalted in judgment** [*downward ascent: embracing the cross for our sake*], and **the holy** [*eros-free, Self-less*] **God will show Himself holy in righteousness** [*e.g. the Trinity embodied in a Man will fulfill Their own law among men*]. Then **lambs** [*newborns re-gene-rating as self-sharers*] will graze as in their pasture, and strangers [*emigrants*] will eat in the waste places of the wealthy [*lit. the fat; e.g. takers who refuse to share*] (Isa. 15:5).

Christ Jesus is both "the Son of God" and "the Son of Man"; the incarnated Son brought God and man together in relational fusion *within* Himself as **the God-Man Nucleus—the Equalizer**. God came down among human beings in Christ, and human beings were lifted up into God in Christ: "God… raised us up with Him, and seated us with Him in the heavenly places in Christ Jesus" (Eph. 2:6). This does not mean we believers become gods ourselves nor are we equal with God; rather, we are "children of God, and if children, heirs also, heirs of God and fellow heirs with Christ" (Rom. 8:17). Father, Son, and Spirit have made us **coequal sharers** of "all the fullness" of Their own shared life in and through the incarnated Son of God who shared His own body with us as the Son of Man and was exalted back into the Triune-life with you and me "in Him." Paul explained:

> Although He existed in the form of God [*one of three eternal Primaries*], He did not consider [*calculate*] **equality** with God a thing to be grasped [*e.g. in entitlement, self-worth-ship*], but **emptied Himself**, taking on the form of a bond-servant, and being made in the likeness of men [*the Son of Man*]. Being found in the appearance of a man [*"the last Adam" 1 Cor. 15:45*], He **humbled** Himself by becoming obedient to the point of death, even death on a cross. For this reason God highly **exalted** Him [*along with us who are incorporated "members" of His corpus*]… (Phil. 2:6-9).

The prophets repeatedly foretold that God would come among men on the earth in a human Messiah; however, when God came in Christ, the religious Jews "did not receive Him" (John 1:11). "Jesus answered them, 'My Father is working until now, and I Myself am working.' For this reason the Jews were seeking all the more to kill Him, because He… was calling God His own Father, making Himself **equal** with God" (John 5:17-19).

As the God-Man Nucleus Who embodies within Himself Father, Spirit, and human beings, the eternal

Son was **exalted in downward ascent** via the cross. Conversely, the created archangel 'Lucifer' became an individualist, "the father of the lie," by **falling in upward descent**: "I will ascend to heaven, I will raise my throne above the stars of God…. **I will make myself like** [*equal to*] **the Most High**" (Isa. 14:13-14). In jealousy-for us, the Triune-God came in Christ among fallen human beings held captive by the false-father in order to lift us into Themselves as "sons [*and daughters*] of the Most High" (Luke 6:35). See how the Triune-God **descended** to human beings in and through Christ:

> **Jesus** [*Nucleus of God Most High*] **came down** with the disciples **and stood on a level place** [*in coequality with man as "the Son of Man"*]; and there was a large crowd of His disciples and a great throng of people…who had come to hear Him and to be healed of their diseases…. And all the people were trying to **touch Him** [*the Trinity made Themselves accessible to man in a human Nucleus*], for **power** [*the fusion 'yield' of three sacrificial Self-sharers*] **was coming from Him** [*from Man to man*] **and healing them all** [*with no partiality or prequalification process to receive: distributive justice*] (Luke 6:17).

Father, Son, and Spirit came as humble, sacrificial Self-sharers in the Nucleus of Christ—

"God in Christ"—standing *within* the Man Jesus on equal ground with mankind for the sole purpose of imparting to us Their own way of coequality in Agape. Isaiah prophesied, "For a Child will be born to us, a Son will be given to us; and the government [*kingdom: cohabitation of God and men*] will rest on His shoulders; and His name will be called Wonderful Counselor [*Spirit*], Mighty God [*All-Three-Mighty*], Eternal Father, Prince of Peace" (Isa. 9:6). See how the Equalizer taught the Trinity-like way of coequality to men:

> An argument [*relational fission*] started among the disciples as to which of them might be the **greatest**. But Jesus, knowing the reasoning in their heart [*eros rationale: calculative self-worth-ship*], **took a child and stood him by His side** [*illustrating coequality*], and said to them, "Whoever receives this child in My name receives Me, and whoever receives Me [*the God-Man Nucleus*] receives Him [*the Triune-God*] who sent Me; for the one who is **least** among all of you, this is the one who is **great**" (Luke 9:46-48).

Since the Man Jesus is "the image of the invisible God" (Col. 1:15), and "the exact representation of His nature" (Heb. 1:3), as we magnify Christ we discover God—Father, Son, and Spirit—is three humble, childlike Persons.

This is the essence of the **divine sovereignty** [*e.g. God as King and Judge*]…What Christ, the incarnate God, did in time, God does and must do in eternity. If Christ is weak and humble on earth [*a childlike Self-sharer*], then God is weak and humble [*three childlike Self-sharers*] in heaven" (C. E. Rolt, *The World's Redemption*, p. 27)

Isaiah's primary theme is the "God of justice" and how the Trinity purposed to come among corrupt mankind in the Equalizer. The eternal Son of God spoke the following words in Isaiah's hearing, then, over 700 years later, He came as the Son of Man and read them from Isaiah's book!

The Spirit of the Lord God is upon Me [*fusion of Spirit and Father in the Son*], because He has anointed Me to preach **the gospel to the poor** [*invitation to "become rich" in the Nucleus of God Most High*]. He has sent Me to proclaim **release to the captives** [*snared as opportunists in Worthless' marketplace*], and recovery of **sight to the blind** [*self-focused: "if your eye is bad…" Mt. 6:23*], to **set free those who are oppressed** [*every man is both a victim and perpetrator of corruption and injustice*], to proclaim **the favorable year of the Lord** [*the Equalizer entering Worthless' world with distributive justice*] (Luke 4:18; Isa. 61:1).

To set captives free, the Equalizer must confront the false-father's de-gene-rate, eros nature and corrupt spirit of self-exaltation that operate in and through human beings compelling us to oppress and exploit one another as opportunists. John made clear, "The Son of God appeared [*as the Son of Man*] for this purpose, to **destroy the works of the devil**" (1 John 3:8). These works operate in and through human beings who are unsuspecting slaves and pawns of the false-father—agents of fission. Believers who assume God has deputized them as law-enforcement officers often misinterpret and misapply Jesus' radical declaration, "Do not think I came to bring **peace** on the earth [*e.g. to tolerate Worthless' status quo hierarchy among men*]; I did not come to bring peace, but a **sword**" (Matt. 10:34).

The sword of the Equalizer is not the blade of a law-enforcement officer deputized to *react* against violators or the weapon of a revolutionary crafted to slaughter those who oppose his new regime. Jesus' sword is a **surgeon's scalpel**—a *proactive* instrument used to perform **invasive surgery** within each human being: "For the word of God [*Triune-Agape in Christ*] is living and active and sharper than any **two-edged sword**, and **piercing** as far as the division of soul and spirit, of both joints and marrow, and able to judge the thoughts and intentions of the heart" (Heb. 4:12).

This razor-sharp **scalpel** is Jesus *Himself*—"a Son made perfect forever" (Heb. 7:28)—the Prototype

Self-sharing Man in whose exact "**image**" God has predestined us all "to become **conformed** [*morphed*]" (Rom. 8:29) and "**made perfect** [*lit. telios: mature; e.g. fuse-able*]" (Heb. 11:40). Internally, "through His **Spirit** who dwells in you" (Rom. 8:11), **Father** masterfully wields the precise, invasive "sword" of His well-pleasing **Son** to systematically **excise** our de-gene-rate, *eros* DNA by which we are enslaved in con-fusion to the false-father Worthless and his world. Simultaneously, the Spirit of Christ (*the Re-gene-rator*), replaces our corrupt DNA with Christ's own incorruptible nature. Salvation is essentially gene-replacement therapy, and we are the "workmanship" of three, collaborative Surgeons!

4. "Jesus called them to Himself"

In his gospel, Matthew recounted how the Equalizer came to embody and equitably distribute justice:

> The mother of the sons of Zebedee came to Jesus with her sons [*James and John*].... She said to Him, "Command that in Your kingdom these two sons of mine may sit one on Your right and one on Your left."...And hearing this, the ten [*other disciples, including Matthew*] became **indignant** [*reactionary*] with the two brothers.
>
> But **Jesus called them to Himself** [*into the*

Nucleus of three Self-sharers: the proactive Equalizer] and said, "You know that the rulers of the Gentiles lord it over them, and their great men exercise authority over them [*Worthless' world hierarchy: upward descent*]. It is not this way among you [*you, who I am not ashamed to "call brothers" Heb. 2:11*], but whoever wishes to become **great** among you shall be your **servant**, and whoever wishes to be **first** among you shall be your **slave** [*Trinity-likeness: downward ascent*]; just as the Son of Man did not come to be **served**, but to **serve** [*as a sacrificial Self-sharer*], and to **give His life a ransom for many**" (Matt. 20:20-28).

In chapter 20 of his gospel, Matthew intentionally coupled together the account above with Jesus' parable of the landowner distributing equal wages to laborers who worked varying lengths of time (Matt. 20:1-16). Matthew was formerly a tax collector before Jesus found him "sitting in the tax booth and said, '**Follow Me**'" (Luke 5:27). Having been trained as a calculative opportunist to use "the deceitfulness of wealth [*lit. mammon*]" (Matt. 13:22) for self-advancement, it seems Jesus' new, revolutionary economy of coequality and justice made quite an impression on him! Matthew also cherished and preserved for us these words of Jesus:

But do not be called Rabbi; for **One is your Teacher** [*the Holy Spirit: Mentor, Wonderful*

Counselor], **and you are all brothers** [*coequals: "be imitators of God as beloved children (re-gene-rating in one bloodline) and walk in (practice) Agape" Eph. 5:1*]. Do not call anyone on earth your father; for **One is your Father**, He who is in heaven. Do not be called leaders; for **One is your Leader**, that is, **Christ** [*the Son: sacrificial Self-sharing God-Man, the Equalizer*]. But the **greatest** among you shall be your **servant**. Whoever exalts himself shall be humbled [*upward descent*]; and whoever humbles himself shall be exalted [*downward ascent*] (Matt. 23:8-12).

In many ways, Jesus' twelve disciples were a sample demographic of all humanity, representing all the varieties of cultural backgrounds, vocational influences, flawed temperaments, and corrupt motivations that you and I and other believers still manifest today. Among the twelve, James and John were reactionary "sons of thunder" (Mark 3:17); Peter was a self-absorbed, self-confident type A personality; Matthew was a calculative, opportunistic tax-collector; Simon the Zealot was a nationalist revolutionary; Judas Iscariot was a pilferer with serious mammon issues; Thomas was a stubborn rationalist; and Jesus was amazed to discover Nathaniel was "an Israelite, indeed, in whom there is no deceit!" (John 1:47). Further, Mary Magdalene was formerly a prostitute oppressed by seven demons, and even Jesus' own mother and brothers "went out to take custody of Him…saying, 'He has lost His senses'" (Mark 3:21).

There is only one possible way that human beings like you and me can cohabit together in true freedom, gen-uine coequality, and sustained peace, and that is **in the Nucleus of the Equalizer** Who invites each of us to become incorporated into Himself as coequal "members" of His own corpus: one new, many-membered Man. Life in relational fusion and inter-personal oneness is only possible "in Christ" the God-Man Nucleus; therefore, **Jesus calls each and all of us into Himself—into the demilitarized zone of Triune-Agape** where we are taught not to devalue, disown, and exploit one another.

Outside of this tested, perfected, sacrificial Self-sharing Man, we exist in a **war zone** of relational fission, corruption, opportunism, injustice, and death. "Father rescued us from the domain of darkness [*relational fission*], and transferred us to the kingdom of His beloved Son [*lit. the Son of His Agape; e.g. relational fusion in the Equalizer*]" (Col. 1:13). Our **corporate transfer** into the Equalizer is the fulfillment of the purpose of the coming of God in Christ:

Caiaphas [*the high priest*] prophesied that Jesus was going to die [*as a sacrificial Self-sharer*] for the nation, and not for the nation

[*Jews*] only, but that He might **gather into one** [*one Nucleus, one body, one cohabitation, "one new man": one kingdom*] **the children of God who are scattered abroad** [*in fission: individualism, tribalism, nationalism, racism, denominationalism, etc.*] (John 11:51-52).

In each of his epistles, Paul clearly spelled out the practical implications of sharing one life together as coequals fused into the Equalizer, and how the Spirit of Christ is ever calling you and me into Himself. "Masters, grant to your slaves **justice** and **fairness**, knowing that you too have a **Master** [*the Equalizer*] in heaven" (Col. 4:1). In a sense, masters and slaves are also managers and employees, commanders and troops, elders and constituents, and even parents and children. Paul's exhorted the Ephesian believers:

Slaves [*e.g. employees, soldiers, children*], be obedient to those who are your **masters** [*e.g. bosses, commanders, parents*] according to the flesh, with fear and trembling, in the sincerity of your heart [*eros-free*], as to Christ [*the Head of our many-membered body*]; not by way of eye-service, as **men-pleasers** [*avoiding penalty and calculating gain*], but as **slaves of Christ** [*"the Agape of Christ controls us"*], doing the will of God from the heart [*yielding to the internal law of our Triune-God*]. With good will **render service**, **as to the Lord**

[*three humble Self-sharers*], **and not to men** [*opportunists*], knowing that whatever good [*gene-rous, sacrificial self-sharing*] thing each one does [*regardless of the losses incurred*], this he will **receive back** from the Lord, whether slave or free.

And **masters**, do the same things to them, and **give up threatening** [*e.g. policing, categorizing, voicing manipulative judgments*], knowing that **both their Master and yours** [*the Equalizer*] **is in heaven**, and there is **no partiality** [*lit. face; e.g. promoting a high-ranking face above a subordinate's face*] **with Him** (Eph. 6:5-9).

5. Exposing 'Even-steven'

The justice of our Triune-God is not man's eros calculation of 'fairness.' I recall that my understanding of justice as a child was not only inadequate, but warped; the way we de-gene-rate, corrupt kids enforced justice and equality was called "**even-steven**." Many heated arguments and offenses arose regarding how that non-negotiable "law" should be interpreted and properly applied to the rules of our games and sharing toys. These irresolvable situations typically degenerated into an exercise of "the survival of the fittest"—the eldest and strongest among us simply got their own way while ignoring the protests of the rest. As "responsible" adults, has anything really changed?

Man-made equality is what we as children used to call "**even-steven**." In a poorly-masked ploy to secure an advantage *for* "me," I would attempt to enforce this "law" exclaiming, "Fair's fair!" But is our "fair" really fair? As an individualist, I do not cry "Even-steven!" and "Fair's fair!" because I am concerned that others receive an equal portion, rather I want more *for* "me." Even-steven is a **forced fairness born of eros calculation** that does not give Father, Son, and Spirit room simply to give or not give as They choose.

Trusting in the **integrity** of The Equalizer and His ability to implement distributive justice and **integrate** us into Himself as coequals, we must set our gene-rous Master absolutely free to do what appears, at present, to be grossly unfair to "me." **Accepting** His seemingly unjust decision by faith is an unspeakable delight both to Him and to the Father of our Lord Jesus Christ. If we simply trust and embrace what appears to be an immediate, sustained loss, in time each of us will discover "Him who is able to do exceedingly abundantly beyond what we could ask or think" (Eph. 3:20).

Someone in the crowd said to Him, "Teacher, **tell my brother to divide the family inheritance with me** [*e.g. even-steven*]." But Jesus said to him, "Man who appointed Me a judge or arbiter over you?" [*e.g. the counterfeit* *equality you seek I cannot give you*]. Then He said to them, "Beware, and be on your guard against every form of greed [*often camouflaged by an equality-crusade, e.g. communism: 'Give us all more' = 'Give me more'*]; for not even when one has an abundance does his **life** consist of possessions [*a kingdom shareholder is not rich in material possessions and rank, but in sharing itself as a "fellow heir" of the Family estate*] (Luke 12:13-15).

In 1994, God engaged me with this life-changing invitation: "Will you father My children?" Because of the sustained sacrifices and longsuffering God knew would be required of me as a self-sharer with Him in this work, His word came to me as an invitation and not as a command. Paul willingly embraced a similar life-lab:

We proved to be gentle among you, as a nursing **mother** tenderly cares for her own children…. We were well-pleased to impart to you not only the gospel of God but also **our own lives** [*sacrificial self-sharing*]…. We were exhorting and encouraging and imploring each one of you as a **father** would his own children, so that you would walk in a manner worthy of the God who calls you into His own kingdom and glory (1 Thess. 2:7-12).

The sovereign manner in which our Triune-God chose each orphaned child from Ukraine and Uganda whom He entrusted to my wife and me and the way He extravagantly loved, faithfully nurtured, and conscientiously mentored these children who were not only considered worthless but a liability by the societies into which they were born has opened wide to me the economy of the kingdom: "**the last shall be first and the first last**" (Matt. 20:16).

Sharing one life in this micro-model of the kingdom called *Father's House Uganda*, we seek to do all things at the Spirit's prompting because we are ever conscious that **the Equalizer's economy of equality** (coequality) **is radically different than ours**. Sometimes when we want to give, the Spirit "forbids" it (Acts 16:6), and on other occasions when it does not seem appropriate to give in our estimation, He says, "Give." Some of the most extravagant, sacrificial gifts Father has moved me to give were to those who hated and persecuted us and whom I naturally considered unworthy, while He sometimes prevented me from helping other beloved friends whom I considered deserving and in need. Clearly, **eros has severely warped my perception of equality, fairness, and justice**.

However, practicing responsive obedience in blind faith (not demanding from God any explanation or proof), while grasping nothing and "standing under" Him with "**a hearing heart**" (1 Ki. 3:9), is enabling me to exchange my corrupt economy of equality for His incorruptible economy of coequality. Paul observed, "the foolishness of God is wiser than men, and the weakness of God is stronger than men" (1 Cor. 1:25). In the same way, the judgments of God that appear inequitable and seem unfair are more just, equitable, and fair than man's most sophisticated calculations of equality and our most conscientious attempts at fairness. For example:

> Thus says the Lord God, "This shall be the boundary by which you shall divide the land for an **inheritance** among the twelve tribes of Israel; **Joseph shall have two portions**. You shall divide it for an inheritance, **each one equally with the other** [*lit. like his brother*]..." (Ezek. 47:13-14).

Over 450 years after Joseph was sold as a slave by his own brothers, and he fulfilled God's purpose "to preserve many people alive" (Gen. 50:20) through a seven-year famine. He even provided abundant grain, anonymously and without cost, to his treacherous brothers and their offspring as coequals; **God justly and equitably compensated Joseph** and his descendants. From age 17 to 30 Joseph was exiled in Egypt before Pharaoh summoned him from the prison and God highly exalted him. Countless times through these thirteen years, Joseph **wrestled with God's apparent unfairness** and the bitter sense

God had forgotten him: "They afflicted his feet with fetters, he himself was laid in irons; until the time that his word came to pass, **the word of the Lord tested him**" (Ps. 105:18-19).

In spite of betrayal, false accusation, and the indifference and forgetfulness of self-absorbed men whom he ministered to, Joseph chose to practice unwavering trust in the God of justice and to serve Him day by day as a sacrificial self-sharing steward. Knowing the corrupt, calculating nature of man and the power of fraternal envy, it is certain the other eleven tribes of Israel stumbled and grumbled over Joseph's **double portion** considering it was compensation for something a man, whom they had never met, did over four centuries before! Nevertheless, **God always repays equitably and without partiality**. Jesus described the equitable economy of "the kingdom of heaven":

> For it is just like a man [*God in Christ*]... who called his own slaves and **entrusted** his possessions to them [*God invests "capital" into de-gene-rate slaves to transform them into gene-rous stewards and heirs*]. To one he gave five talents [*75 years wages; one talent = 15 years wages of a laborer*], to another two [*30 years wages*], and to another one [*15 years wages*], **each according to his own ability** [*assessed by the Equalizer*].... Immediately the one who had received the five talents went away and

traded with them and gained five more talents [*e.g. fruit-bearing: investing this "capital" into others and practicing reciprocal gene-rosity as coequals*].... But he who received the one talent...dug a hole in the ground and hid his master's money [*e.g. a slave of self-worth-ship who suppresses and aborts the gene-rous seed of Christ within himself*].

Now after a long time [*e.g. "the Farmer waits" Jas. 5:7*] the master of those slaves came and **settled accounts** [*the day of judgment*].... "Well done good and faithful slave...enter into the joy of your master [*the kingdom: receiving a "full" share as a son, fellow-heir, and co-worker in the one shared estate of three Shareholders and Distributors*]. And the one also who had received the one talent came up and said, "**Master, I knew you to be a hard** [*exacting, inequitable*] **man**, reaping where you did not sow and gathering where you scattered no seed [*I calculated you to be a shrewd opportunist*]. And I was afraid, and went and hid your talent.... See, you have what is yours."

But his master answered, "**You wicked** [*faith-less*], **lazy** [*fruit-less*] **slave** ...Take away the talent from him, and give it to the one who has the ten talents." [*Luke 19:25 adds: "...his* servants answered, 'Master, he has ten talents already'" meaning, "Is that fair?"] For **to everyone who has** [*e.g. receives the "investment capital" of God's gene-rous love and multiplies it by sacrificially sharing himself with others*], **more shall be given**, and he will have an **abundance** [*heirs of God*]; but from the **one who does not have, even what he does have** [*and does not faithfully cherish*] **shall be taken away** (Matt. 25:14-29).

6. Jesus Out-socialists the Socialists

Oswald Chambers received profound insight into the Equalizer and how the distributive justice of our Triune-God is embodied in Him and revealed through Him. Chambers made this bold declaration:

> **Jesus Christ out-socialists the socialists**.... The ecclesiastical idea of a servant of God [*e.g. the hierarchical authority structure of the world adopted and practiced by the church*] is not Jesus Christ's idea.... Jesus says that in His kingdom he that is greatest shall be **the servant of all**.... The real test of a saint is not preaching the gospel but **washing disciples' feet** (Chambers, *My Utmost For His Highest*, Feb. 25).

The basic premise of socialism is that citizens, as **equals**, must share both the responsibility (input) and the rewards (output) of their cohabitation **equitably**. Distributive justice has been the alleged aim and apparent claim of countless socialist initiatives, which men have proposed and attempted, yet it has never actually worked anywhere on the earth! In **counter-reaction** to the tyranny and oppression of self-exalting, self-indulgent kings, czars, emperors, and chief executives in various corners of the world, each generation of de-gene-rate mankind has become rapt with lofty aspirations of equality and labored to establish their own version of '**even-steven**' **socialism**.

However, after overthrowing the former administration (usually by violence) and setting up new external laws and systems of law-enforcement, each of these new, eros-infected regimes de-gene-rated into corruption and precipitated even greater tyranny and injustice, which in turn, exponentially multiplied the inequality and poverty. Accurate world-historians and political scientists consider distributive justice to be an unattainable, utopian idea since they cannot cite a single **socialist experiment** that had sustained success in fulfilling its' original aims.

In my lifetime, I have travelled to more than 60 nations and been a resident in the United States, Hong Kong (China), the former Soviet nation of Ukraine, and Uganda. I have witnessed the phenomenon of socialist counter-reaction and its counter-productive outcome in many places on all continents. Man-made socialism is actually just capitalism masked by the hypocrisy of a handful of committee members who together usurped the position and privileges of the solitary czar or emperor whom they ousted.

Socialism and distributive justice simply do not work unless the *internal* law of Agape is written into each citizen—***gen-uine* coequality**. True justice had to **come down** to fallen, *de-gene-rate*, reactionary, self-exalting, opportunistic human beings from Father, Son, and Spirit Who made Themselves our **Servants** and **burden-Bearers** in the *gene-rous* God-Man Jesus. In the cohabitation of the kingdom of God, there are foundations of **true, eros-free socialism**, which Father, Son, and Spirit actually lived out among fallen, corrupt men through the incorruptible Man Jesus and continue to live out through the Spirit of Christ among us today.

As humble, sacrificial Self-sharers, Father, Son, and Spirit honor and serve One Another as **Coequals** according to the internal law of Agape. Via **downward ascent**, Each of these Eternals exalts and adds to the other Two by His own Self-expenditure; therefore, Father, Son, and Spirit are **collectively exalted** as "God Most High" (Psa. 57:2; Acts 7:48). In and through Christ Jesus, our Triune-God intentionally chose **the lowly, practical chore of washing feet** to reveal the nature and extent of Their own reciprocal care for One Another and to demonstrate for human beings the practical activity of Their own shared life in coequality. This particular lowly chore uniquely summarized how God in Christ "out-socialists the socialists"!

Jesus, knowing that the Father had given **all things** into His hands [*as a Steward-Son, the God-Man Nucleus*], and that He had come forth from God and was going back to God, got up from supper, and **laid aside His garments** [*His own autonomy and individuality as the Son*]; and taking a towel He **girded Himself** [*with Triune-Agape: permitting all three humble Eternals to share Themselves with mankind through His own Self-emptying*]. Then He poured water into the basin, and began to **wash the disciples' feet and to wipe them with the towel with which He was girded**....

When Jesus had...taken His garments and reclined at the table again, He said to them, **"Do you know what I have done to you?** [*I have shown you the Triune-Root of "true" justice*] You call Me Teacher and Lord, and you are right, for so **I AM** [*the Nucleus of three eternal Self-sharers*]. If I then, the Lord [*Creator*] and the Teacher [*Prototype Man*] washed your feet, **you ought to wash one another's feet**. For I gave you an **example** [*of the "Us"*] that you also [*as a Trinity-like reciprocal self-sharers*] should do as I did to you" (John 13:3-15).

Through this act of Self-emptying, Self-sharing humility, Christ Jesus, who is the Nucleus of the Triune-God, opened Himself wide to us—"I AM the door" (John 10:9)—allowing us to see into Him and **observe** "**the way**" Father, Son, and Spirit cohabit together within Christ and "**the way**" you and I must enter and participate together in the kingdom of God. In and through the Son Jesus and "the Spirit of His Son," Father Himself runs out to meet us lost, orphaned children and receive us even when we are corrupt, filthy, con-fused, and in trouble (see John 15:20); **Father Himself washes our feet**. In order for us to enter and embody the kingdom on the earth as **coequal** "**members**" **of Christ**, we must fulfill the law of Agape as "imitators of God"; we must humble ourselves and learn to care for one another's practical needs in a Trinity-like way.

Seven-hundred years before God came on the earth in human flesh, the prophet Isaiah foretold how "Immanuel...God with us" (Isa. 7:14; Matt. 1:23) would gird Himself in this very way as a humble Self-sharer to unveil the eternal Root of Triune-Justice and inaugurate Their eternal kingdom of freedom and coequality among men:

> Then a **shoot** will spring from the **root** of Jesse [*Jesus, "son of David"*], and a **branch** from his roots will **bear fruit** [*re-gene-rate human beings as a new creation*]. The Spirit of the Lord will rest on Him [*fused into the Son: the*

God-Man Nucleus], the Spirit of wisdom and understanding [*Agape rationale*], the Spirit of counsel and of strength [*fusion power*], the Spirit of knowledge and the fear of the Lord [*the way of Triune-Agape: jealousy-for*].

He will not judge by what His eyes see [*partiality: "man looks at the outward appearance but God looks at the heart" 1 Sam. 16:7*], **nor make a decision by what His ears hear** [*deference to smooth talkers*]; **but with righteousness** [*as the Equalizer*] **He will judge the poor**, and decide with **fairness** [*distributive justice*] for the afflicted of the earth; and He will strike the earth with the rod of His mouth [*the non-negotiable law of Agape*], and with the breath of His mouth [*Vortex of the Triune-Pneuma*] He will slay the wicked [*lawless opportunists*]. Also **righteousness** [*sacrificial Self-sharing*] **will be the belt about His loins**, and **faithfulness** [*relational altruism*] **the belt about His waist** [*e.g. "and taking a towel, He girded Himself…and began washing the disciples feet"*] (Isa. 11:1-10).

The profound revelation of the law of Agape and Triune-Justice is in this lowly act of foot-washing. Further, it affords us deeper insight into the meaning of Jesus' words to Peter:

So He came to Simon Peter. He said to Him, "Lord, do you wash my feet?" Jesus answered and said to him, "**What I do** [*unveiling and demonstrating "justice and the Agape of God" Luke 11:42*], **you do not realize now**, but you will understand hereafter [*at Pentecost Peter was fused with other believers into one body in one Spirit*]." Peter said to Him, "Never shall you wash my feet!" Jesus answered him, "**If I do not wash you** [*of individualism, corruption, lawlessness, opportunism, categorizing, etc.*], **you have no part with Me** [*you are not fit to be incorporated as a sharer in My many-membered corpus in Whom the Trinity and human beings cohabit together*]" (John 13:6-8).

Distributive justice, which is the **proactive** 'yield' of *gen-uine* coequality, is the most obvious feature that distinguishes the cohabitation of the kingdom of God from all **reactionary**, man-made governments, communities, associations, and institutions. Proceeding forth from corrupt, *de-gene-rate* man, socialism is doomed from inception to hypocrisy, futility, failure, famine, and totalitarian oppression. Proceeding forth from God in Christ—"the Rock" of Triune-solidarity—kingdom socialism flourishes with coequality, distributive justice, freedom, and bounty.

Even in ancient times, Abraham recognized Worthless' design and reactionary influence operating in and through the man-made kingdoms of his day; therefore, "he was looking for the city [*cohabitation*] which has **foundations** [*the Rock of Christ: the Equalizer*], whose **architect and builder is God** [*three sacrificial Self-sharers in coequality*]" (Heb. 11:10). When Jesus came, He stated plainly, "**My kingdom is not of this world**" (John 18:36). In the Equalizer's eros-free cohabitation, God chooses, cherishes, and champions the weak:

> For consider your calling, brethren [*children re-gene-rating in one bloodline*], that there were **not many wise** according to the flesh, not many **mighty**, not many **noble**; but God has chosen the **foolish** things of the world to shame the wise, and God has chosen the **weak** things of the world to shame the things which are strong, and the **base** things of the world and **the despised God has chosen** [*to join Him in downward ascent*], the things that are not, so that He may nullify the things that are [*Worthless' hierarchical structures*], so **that no man may boast** [*manifest self-worth-ship*] **before God** [*three humble Eternals*].

> But by His doing you are **in Christ Jesus** [*incorporated as coequal members into the corpus of the Equalizer*], who became to us wisdom from God, and righteousness and sanctification and redemption, so that, just as it is written, "Let him who boasts, boast in

the Lord [*You are the Rock of my salvation*]" (1 Cor. 1:26-31).

Our Triune-God came among human beings in Christ—*The Equalizer*—as the Forerunner of all *true* revolutionaries. In an age of capricious, oppressive rulers, the founding fathers of the United States were inspired by a vision of God to compose and sign **The Declaration of Independence** at the cost of their own lives; below is an excerpt:

> We hold these truths to be self-evident [*derived from our Triune-Creator: the "Us"*], that **all men are created equal** [*made in the image and likeness of three Coequals who are one in Agape*], that they are endowed by their Creator with certain **unalienable Rights** [*the gift of individuality and free will is essential to coequality and inter-personal fusion in Agape*], that among these are Life, Liberty and the pursuit of happiness [*which do not exist in individualism, but only in reciprocal self-sharing*]. That to secure these rights, Governments are instituted among men, deriving their **just powers** [*invested authority*] from the consent of the governed.

Though the attempt of these colonists to establish a free society of **coequals** was immature and deeply flawed in many ways, it has been cherished and revered by millions who flooded its safe harbor—"*In God We Trust.*" Of course, the **hypocrisy** of racism, the ongoing practice of slavery, and aggressively displacing the Indian tribes indigenous to the Americas, while proclaiming "all men are created equal," makes evident that we all have serious *de-gene-rate* issues. Maturing together in the image and likeness of the Equalizer is a lengthy process of *re-gene-ration*, re-education, and acculturation!

The Declaration of Independence served as an antecedent to *The Constitution of the United States*, and in this **iterative process** of refining law and distributive justice, **twenty-seven subsequent *Amendments*** were made to this legal framework. Must we believers make a similar onward journey to cultivate and preserve freedom and coequality? Isaiah wrote:

> We have a **strong city** [*"we receive a kingdom which cannot be shaken" Heb.12:28*], **He sets up walls and ramparts for security** [*God is "fitting together" sacrificial self-sharers as "living stones": coequals who lay down their lives for one another*]. Open the gates that **the righteous nation may enter** [*"imitators of God" incorporated together into the corpus of "God is a dwelling place"*], the one that remains **faithful** [*altruism toward God and one another tested and proven in battle*].... For in God, the Lord, we have **an everlasting Rock** [*the God-*

Man Jesus: Cornerstone of Triune-Solidarity]
(Isa. 26:1-4).

Man-made cohabitations (communes) of
socialism are comprised of *de-gene-rate* individualists
who are not *gen-uinely* **integrated** (fused) with
one another into the unshakable Nucleus. The
cohabitation is "built on the **sand**" rather than "built
on the **rock** [*relational solidarity*]" (Matt. 7:24-27).
Paul urged us believers to esteem one another as
coequals in worth and function, "so that there may
be **no division** [*disintegration, relational fission*]
in the body [*the corpus of Christ*], **but that the
members may have the same care for one another**
[*coequals practicing reciprocal gene-rosity as sacrificial
self-sharers*]" (1 Cor. 12:25).

The Equalizer Christ Jesus, who is the Nucleus
of the Trinity, was torn open on the cross in the
presence of corrupt, self-focused individualists for
this reason: to grant us opportunity to see how,
within Christ, Father, Son, and Spirit share one
nature, one name, one cohabitation, one purpose,
and one life according to the internal law of
Agape. Father, Son, and Spirit desire for Their own
"abundant life" to be manifested in each of us
individually and among us collectively as Their re-
gene-rated children: "Then God said, 'Let **Us** [*three
Coequals*] make man in Our image [*a created 'us' in
relational coequality*] according to Our [*sacrificial Self-
sharing*] likeness, and let them **rule** [*e.g. as coequals*

who implement Our distributive justice]…'" (Gen. 1:26). John received a *Revelation* of this resurrected, ascended Equalizer:

> You were slain and purchased for God with Your blood **mankind from every tribe and tongue and people and nation** [*adopted into one Family, re-gene-rated into one bloodline*]. You have made them to be a kingdom [*"heirs of God, fellow heirs with Christ": fellow-citizens*] and priests to our God; and they will reign on the earth [*e.g. as coequals who implement the distributive justice of three Coequals*].… I looked, and behold, a great multitude which no one could count, from **every nation and all tribes and peoples and tongues, standing** [*coequally*] **before the throne** and before the Lamb [*the Equalizer*], clothed in white robes… (Rev. 5:9-10; 7:9).

After Jesus' resurrection and ascension, Father and Son gave us an infinite gift—**sacrificial Spirit-sharing Love**: "You were sealed in Christ [*as coequal "members" of His corpus*] with **the Holy Spirit of promise**, who is given as a pledge [*lit. down-payment*] of our **inheritance**" (Eph. 1:13-14). The Person of the Holy Spirit is also called "the Spirit of your Father" (Matt. 10:20); "the Spirit of His Son" (Gal. 4:6); and "the Spirit of God…the Spirit of Christ" (Rom. 8:9). In and through the Person of the Holy Spirit, all three Coequals abide within each one of us **individually**, and all three Coequals abide in the midst of us **collectively**, that is, in the midst of our relational, inter-personal oneness in Christ. See how our proactive Triune-God "out-socialists the socialists":

> I will pour out My Spirit on **all mankind** [*coequally*]; and your **sons** and your **daughters** will prophesy [*no gender discrimination*], your **old** men will dream dreams, your **young** men will see visions [*no age discrimination*]. Even on the **male** and **female servants** [*no socio-economic, class, or racial discrimination*] I will pour out My Spirit [*the "down-payment" of Our kingdom of freedom and coequality*] in those days (Joel 2:28-29).

7. Judged Through a Man

In the first-century world, the epicenter of secular and religious philosophy was the Aeropagus on Mars Hill in Athens, Greece, and the influence of ideas exchanged there resounded around the globe. Luke noted, "Now all the Athenians and the strangers visiting there used to spend their time in nothing other than telling or hearing something new" (Acts 17:21). Among the elite philosophers gathered there, Paul made this profound declaration: **"God has fixed a day in which He will judge the world in righteousness through a Man..."** (Acts

17:31).

In this study, we have learned many things about what the law and judgment of God is not, and we have been challenged to surrender many misconceptions. Now we must understand what God's judgment actually is. Seven centuries before Paul unveiled God's "**Standard**" of judgment in Athens, God spoke to the prophet Jeremiah:

> Roam to and fro through the streets of Jerusalem [*reputed to be "the holy (eros-free) city"*], and look now and take note. And seek in her open squares if you can **find a man**, if there is **one who does justice** [*champions the freedom and coequality of all*], **who seeks truth** [*lit. faithfulness; relational altruism*], then I will **pardon her** (Jer. 5:1).

The Scriptures often refer to the city of Jerusalem as a "**her**" because God established this cohabitation through King David as a prophetic type (an earthly rehearsal studio) of "the **holy city**, the new Jerusalem coming down out of heaven from God, made ready as a [*fused and fuse-able many-membered*] **bride adorned for her husband** [*the Triune-Groom: God in Christ*]" (Rev. 21:2). However, God found that all of the inhabitants of the earthly Jerusalem were corrupt individualists; not even one man could be found who practiced coequality as a sacrificial self-sharer in fusion oneness with others!

Before the foundation of the world, God knew He would have to come Himself in human flesh to be this "**one**" **Man**. God Himself was the only Man capable of fulfilling the vision of this cohabitation of God and men that was revealed to David: "I will cause a righteous **Branch of David** to spring forth [*"Jesus, Son of David" Luke 18:38*]; and He will execute justice and righteousness on the earth [*conquer Worthless' world of inequality, corruption, and injustice*]" (Jer. 33:15). The prophet Isaiah described how this "Son of Man" would embody within Himself infinitely more than could be seen by the natural eye:

> A **Son** will be given to us [*Son of God; Son of Man*]; and **the government** will rest on His shoulders [*the kingdom: cohabitation of God and man within a God-Man*] and His name will be called Wonderful Counselor [*Spirit*], Mighty God [*All-Three-Mighty*], Eternal Father, Prince of Peace.... A **throne** will even be established in **lovingkindness** [*extreme Self-forsaking love*], and a **judge** will sit on it in **faithfulness** [*a Trinity-like Man "made perfect" as a sacrificial Self-sharer*].... Moreover, he will seek **justice** [*coequality and freedom for all*] and be prompt in **righteousness** (Isa. 9:6; 11:3-4; 16:5).

Dwelling in "fullness" within Jesus, the first

incorruptible Man, the eternal Father, Son, and Spirit entered Worthless' world and abided by Their own law among corrupt human beings. By fulfilling that law in Christ, the Triune-God raised a **Standard** of justice in the fallen world—one Man through Whom all other men will be judged:

> **The Lord is righteous within her** [*in the Man Jesus, God entered this cohabitation of individualists and lived among its corrupt citizens*]; **He will do no injustice**. Every morning **He brings justice** [*coequality in Agape*] **to light** [*Christ reveals how we no longer reflect the image and likeness of the "Us" Who created "us"*]; **He does not fail** [*"Agape never fails" 1 Cor. 13:8*]. But **the unjust** [*de-gene-rate opportunists*] **know no shame** [*e.g. "they… crucified the Lord of glory" 1 Cor. 2:8*] (Zeph. 3:5).

Son Made Perfect Forever

The Son Jesus was tested, perfected, and proven to be the one and only *gen-uine* Man, the first of His kind: an incorruptible, sacrificial Self-sharer among all other de-gene-rate, corrupt human beings. God appointed "**a Son made perfect forever**" (Heb. 7:28) to be the living Standard of law, justice, and judgment in Worthless' lawless world. Justice is not a static set of laws; **justice is a dynamic Person**: "God in Christ." Apart from Christ, and "the way" of Triune-Agape, which He Himself embodies, there is no true justice among men. God spoke through Isaiah:

> Pay attention to Me, O My people, and give ear to Me, O My nation; for **a law will go forth from Me** [*"the Son of Father's Agape"* Col. 1:13], and I will **set My justice for a light of the peoples** [*three Coequals dwelling in fusion and 3-D "fullness" in Christ*]. My righteousness is **near** [*"Immanuel, God with us"*], My salvation has gone forth, and **My arms** [*the Son of God and the Spirit of God*] **will judge the peoples**; the coastlands [*Galilee by the Sea*] will wait for Me, and for **My arm** [*"God in Christ": The Equalizer*] they will wait expectantly…. Listen to Me, you who know righteousness [*coequality in Agape*], **a people in whose heart is My law** [*"Christ in you, the hope of glory" Col. 1:27*] (Isa. 51:4-7).

The Man Jesus was not automatically **qualified** to be this Standard "*through*" whom God would judge all men. During His 33 years as a Man on the earth, "Jesus kept increasing in wisdom and stature, and in favor with God and men" (Luke 2:52). The Son of Man practiced abiding in perpetual, relational fusion with Father and Spirit just as He had in eternity as the Son of God. Therefore Paul wrote, "The first man, Adam, became a living soul. The last

Adam [*the Son of Man*] **became a life-giving spirit**" (1 Cor. 15:45).

> But of the Son God says, "Your throne, O God, is forever and ever, and the righteous scepter is the scepter of Your kingdom [*cohabitation*]. You [*the Son of Man*] have **loved righteousness** [*Agape: sacrificial self-sharing*] and **hated lawlessness** [*eros: self-worth-ship*]; therefore God, Your God, has anointed You with the oil of gladness [*"all the fullness of Deity" Col. 2:9*] **above Your companions** [*a Man distinguished among all other human beings*]" (Heb. 1:8-9).

Out from His living union with Father and Spirit and through His own human, life-giving spirit, "Jesus, Son of the Most High God" **humbled Himself** in downward ascent to lift human beings in upward descent. Jesus, the Son of Man, **emptied Himself** to make room for us to be incorporated as coequal members of His own corpus, so we could be raised up in Him and with Him (Eph. 2:6). He washes all our feet coequally; He distributes food to us all coequally; He heals us all coequally; and He lays down His own life for us all coequally. Outside of the tested, proven "Son made perfect" true justice does not exist. 700 years after the prophet Isaiah foretold the coming of this Equalizer among men, Matthew witnessed firsthand the Man Jesus actually fulfill it.

Many followed Him, and **He healed them all** [*coequally*], and warned them not to tell who He was [*distributive justice without a political agenda or campaign of Self-promotion*]. This was to fulfill what was spoken through Isaiah the prophet: "Behold, **My Servant** [*Steward-Son and Heir of all things*] whom I have **chosen** [*as the Nucleus of the fusion of God and man*]; **My Beloved** in whom My soul is **well-pleased** [*to dwell*]; I will put My Spirit upon Him [*Father and Spirit fused into the Son of Man*], and **He shall proclaim justice** [*coequality in Agape*] **to the Gentiles**.

"He will not quarrel, nor cry out; nor will anyone hear His voice in the streets [*no coercive propaganda or external law-enforcement*]. A battered reed [*a vulnerable, oppressed individual*] He will not break off, and a smoldering wick He will not put out, until **He leads justice** [*coequality in Agape*] **to victory** [*Mission Impossible: bringing all mankind into coequality in Agape within Himself not by external coercion, but by internal re-generation: conquering one corrupt individualist at a time*]. And **in His name** the Gentiles will hope [*"crucified with Christ": forfeiting their own autonomous name, identity, and life for a coequal share in His name, identity, and life*]" (Matt. 12:18-21; Isa. 42:1-2).

Jesus testified, "I AM the way and the truth and the life [*of the Triune-God*]…" (John 14:6). The law of Father, Son, and Spirit is embodied within this one, tested, perfected Man. Jesus Himself—"a Son made perfect forever"—is the fulfillment and **Standard** of the law of Triune-Agape among men:

For not even the Father judges anyone, but **He has given all judgment to the Son** [*as a sacrificial Self-sharing Man "made perfect"*], **so that all will honor the Son even as they honor the Father** [*as Coequals; no false hierarchy: "I and the Father are one"*]. He who does not honor the Son does not honor the Father who sent Him…. He who hears My word, and believes Him who sent Me, has eternal life and **does not come into judgment**, but has passed **out of death** [*eros individualism, fission*] **into life** [*relational fusion in the kingdom of God*].

For just as the Father has life [*Agape: life-giving DNA*] in Himself, so He gave to the Son [*as a Man*] also to have life in Himself; and He gave Him **authority to execute judgment because He is the Son of Man** [*"the last Adam"; "firstborn" of a new race of re-gene-rated mankind*]…. For an hour is coming in which all who are in the tombs will hear His voice, and will come forth; those who did the good deeds [*the dead living: sacrificial self-*

sharers] to a resurrection of **life**, those who committed the evil deeds [*the living dead: opportunism, self-indulgence*] to a resurrection of **judgment**. I can do nothing on My own initiative [*autonomously*]. As I hear I judge; and **My judgment is just because I do not seek My own will** [*self-will*], but the will of Him who sent Me….

If anyone hears My sayings and does not keep them, **I do not judge him**; for I did not come to judge the world, but to save the world. He who rejects Me [*the Nucleus of the Trinity*] and does not receive My sayings, has one who judges him; **the word I spoke** [*revelation of Triune-Agape I embodied, taught, modeled, and demonstrated*] **is what will judge him at the last day** (John 5:22-30; 12:47-48).

Victim of Man's Injustice

The internal law of Agape ("the divine nature") was first perfected in the Son of Man so it could be perfected within us. As *de-gene-rate*, corrupt men and women, we recognize and esteem Him as the only *gen-uine*, incorruptible Man and relocate into Him by faith: "**If He would render Himself as a guilt offering, He will see His offspring…**" (Isa. 53:10). Dorothy Sayers described how God's righteous Standard of judgment established in and through the Man Jesus becomes painfully obvious to us self-promoting individualists only as we recognize the way Christ willingly embraced and suffered our oppression, injustice, and corrupt judgment:

> God has created us perfectly **free to disbelieve Him** as much as we choose. If we do disbelieve, then He and we must take the consequences in a world ruled by cause and effect [*sowing and reaping: the fixed law of our Triune-Creator*]....
>
> That **God should play the tyrant over man** is a dismal story of unrelieved oppression [*"the lie": in eros rationale, men blame God for the consequences of their own injustice to one another*]; that **man should play the tyrant over man** is the usual dreary record of human futility [*"the rulers of the Gentiles lord it over them, and their great men exercise authority over them" Matt. 20:25*]; but that **man should play the tyrant over God and find Him** [*God in Christ*] **a better man than himself** [*human as God intended*] is an astonishing drama indeed (Dorothy Sayers, "The Greatest Drama"; *Bread and Wine*, Orbis, 2003, p. 297).

The God-Man Jesus embraced the groundless accusations and indictments of His own people who "disowned" Him, as well as the unjust verdict and death-sentence of Pontius Pilate. "For Christ also died for sins once for all, **the just for the unjust**, so that He might bring us [*de-gene-rates*] to God, having been put to death in the flesh, but **made alive in the spirit** [*"a life-giving spirit": the first fuse-able Man*]" (1 Pet. 3:18). On this basis, Paul made his declaration:

> **God** [*incorruptible Triune-Agape*] **has fixed a day in which He will judge the world** [*e.g. Worthless' hierarchical world populated by eros individualists and oppressed by lawless opportunists*] **in righteousness through a Man** [*Christ Jesus: the embodiment of the law and justice of three Coequals*] **whom He has appointed** [*tested and "made perfect" as the Equalizer*], **having furnished proof** [*that Jesus is incorruptible*] **to all** [*corrupt*] **men by raising Him from the dead** (Acts 17:31).

The power of death and decay is the result of "slavery to **corruption**" (Rom. 8:21) at work in the spirit (*self-worth-ship*), soul (*self-will*), and body (*self-indulgence*) of each and every human being: "**the wages of sin** [*eros individualism*] **is death** [*fission decay*]…" (Rom. 6:23). Corruption manifests itself in the hypocrisy of counterfeit love (*eros*) and opportunism with which we all approach God and one another. As a *gen-uine*, sacrificial Self-sharer, "the Son of Man" embraced death on the cross to absorb into Himself the sins of all us *de-gene-rate* "takers" of the world and to comprehensively exhaust into Himself the power of the curse of our relational fission from God and one another. Jesus said:

Now **judgment** is upon this world; now the ruler of this world [*the false-father Worthless: "the father of the lie"*] will be cast out [*expelled from the hearts and minds (DNA) of human beings one at a time*]. **And I** [*the Equalizer*], **if I AM lifted up from the earth** [*crucified*], **will draw all men to Myself** [*re-gene-rate corrupt, self-exalting individualists and incorporate them as coequal "members" into My resurrected corpus*] (John 12:31-32).

The Son Jesus embraced this death-sentence for our sakes knowing by faith, "You [*Father and Spirit*] will not abandon My soul to Sheol; nor will You allow Your Holy One [*the eros-free Nucleus of Holy, Holy, Holy*] to **undergo decay**" (Psa. 16:10; Acts 13:35). In other words, the Son conquered death as a Man by overcoming Worthless' system of tyranny, "that through death He might render powerless him who had the power of death, that is, the devil, and might free those who through fear of death [*eros instinct of self-preservation*] were subject to slavery [*"slaves of corruption": self-worth-ship*] all their lives" (Heb. 2:14-15). As the consummate overcomer, the Man Jesus was invested with all divine authority:

Christ Jesus [*a Man "made perfect"*], **who is to judge the living and the dead by His appearing and His kingdom** [*Nucleus of relational fusion: unshielded Light*] (2 Tim. 4:1).

Father, Son, and Spirit are called "**the living God**" (Jer. 10:10; 2 Cor. 2:16) because these three Coequals are **alive** to One Another and to us in extreme Self-forsaking love. Consider that "the living and the dead" does not merely refer to one's **physiological** condition, whether my heart is still beating or I am flat-lined and buried. The living are **spiritually alive**; in Christ, the living are "the dead living": dead to self and therefore alive as a sacrificial self-sharer to God and others in Agape. The dead are "the living dead": alive to self and therefore dead to others in eros as an individualist ruled by self-worth-ship. Thomas à Kempis explained:

> Those who hear **the word of the cross** [*co-crucifixion: "lose your life" in individualism to "find it" in relational fusion with others in coequality*] **and follow it willingly now** [*follow Jesus: "I have been crucified with Christ" Gal. 2:20*], **need not fear judgment**.... Everyone who serves the cross [*who deny self-interest to "seek first His"*], who in this life **made themselves one with the Crucified** [*"lays down his own life" to be incorporated into His many-membered corpus*], will draw near with confidence to **Christ, the judge**. Why then do you fear to take up the cross [*embrace the tree of life*] when through it you can win the kingdom?

You will not find a **higher way**, nor a **less exalted** [*self-exalted*] but **safer way**, than the way of the cross [*downward ascent: the way of "Jesus, Son of the Most High God"*]….Realize that **to know Christ you must lead a dying life** [*"if anyone comes after Me, he must deny himself and take up his cross and follow Me"* Matt. 16:24]. The more you die to yourself, the more you will live unto God (Thomas à Kempis, "The Royal Road," from an online edition of *The Imitation of Christ*).

In his Gospel, Luke made a fascinating observation: "They **acknowledged God's justice**, having been **baptized**…" (Luke 7:29). In His own death and resurrection, the Man Jesus provided a "way" for you and me to follow Him in downward ascent. In the watery grave of baptism, I am able to **drown and bury my** "**old self**, which is being corrupted in accordance with the lusts of deceit so that might I may be resurrected with Christ "and **put on the new self**, which in the likeness of God has been created in righteousness and holiness of the truth [*Agape perfected in a Prototype Man and made communicable to us*]" (Eph. 4:22-23).

Only the "new self"—a sacrificial self-sharer "born from above" (John 3:3)—is able to see our Triune-Creator as Coequals in Agape and is able to relate **lawfully** to his brothers and sisters as coequals in Agape. Only the "new self" is able to enter and participate together with others in the fusion of the Trinity: "**baptizing them in** [*fusing them into*] **the name of the Father, and of the Son, and of the Holy Spirit**" (Matt. 28:19). That which meets the living Standard of the Man Jesus Christ and fulfills the law and justice of our Triune-God is none other than the **death-sentence** of my old, corrupt self. I maintain that death by embracing the daily cross so I may be alive to God my Savior and to my brothers and sisters in Christ with whom I share one, Trinity-like life in coequality.

God's Standard of judgment "through a Man" is made simple for us in a promise and in a warning. Jesus **promised**, "All that the Father gives to Me will come to Me, and the one [*individualist*] who comes to Me [*"loses his life for My sake" Matt. 16:25*] I will certainly not cast out [*of My body: the cohabitation of God and man*]" (John 6:37). Jesus **warns** those who persist in individualism and fission and who refuse to lose their autonomous lives into Him and cohabit with others as coequal members of His one body. He will say to them in the judgment, "**I never knew you** [*in My many-membered body*]; depart from Me, you who practice **lawlessness** [*eros: self-worth-ship, opportunism*]" (Matt. 7:23).

Look at Paul's famous declaration in a new way: "there is now **no condemnation for those who are in Christ Jesus**" (Rom. 8:1). In eros rationale ('me'-centered thinking), I misinterpret being "in Christ Jesus" to mean my own personal faith in Christ ('me in Jesus'). In Agape rationale ('us'-centered thinking), my freedom from "condemnation" (exemption from judgment) comes only by abiding in **coequality** together with others "in Christ Jesus" as a sacrificial self-sharing "member" of His one body. If I am not sacrificially sharing myself with my **brother** "in Christ" I am not sharing myself with "**God** in Christ," and I am still subject to judgment under "the **law** of Christ" (Gal. 6:2).

Mirror of God's Glory

What exactly does it mean to be judged "through" the life of the Man Jesus? Barbara Taylor Brown provides a profound answer:

> Jesus offered Himself as a **mirror** they could see themselves in, and they were so appalled by what they saw, they **smashed** it. They smashed Him in every way they could…. Who is it that told me the truth about myself so clearly that I wanted to kill him for it? According to John, Jesus died because He told the truth to everyone He met. He *was* the truth, a perfect mirror in which people saw themselves in God's own light….
>
> In the presence of His **integrity**, our own **pretense** is exposed. In the presence of His **constancy**, our **cowardice** is brought to light. In the presence of His **fierce love** for God and

for us, our own **hardness of heart** is revealed. Take Him out of the room and all those things become relative…but leave Him in the room and there is no room to hide. He is the light of the world. In His presence, people either **fall down to worship Him** or do everything they can to **extinguish His light** (Barbara Brown Taylor, "Truth to Tell," from *The Perfect Mirror*, 1998, Christian Century Foundation).

The Scriptures make clear that neither Father, nor Son, nor Spirit judge us; the essential instrument through which all mankind will be judged is "**the word**" **of God in Christ**, which functions like a "**mirror**." James explained there are two possible responses when each individualist is confronted by his own self-image in this mirror:

If anyone is a hearer [*admirer*] of the word [*the revelation of Triune-Agape in Christ*], and not a doer [*follower*], he is like a man who looks at his **natural face in a mirror** [*the face of his de-gene-rate birth and corrupt nature as an individualist is exposed in the light of the gen-uine Man Jesus*]; for once he has looked at himself and gone away, he has immediately **forgotten what kind of person he was** [*he regresses into self-deception, self-worth-ship*].

But one who looks intently at [*magnifies*]

the perfect law, the law of liberty [*the law of three Coequals Who reciprocate sacrificial Self-sharing love*] and abides by it [*embraces relational coequality and altruism with others*] not having become a forgetful **hearer** [*regressing into self-worth-ship: "suppressing the truth in unrighteousness"*] but an effectual **doer** [*yielding to re-gene-ration in Christ's communicable DNA*], this man will be **blessed** [*as a gen-uine son*] in what he does (James 1:23-25).

The essential instrument through which all mankind will be judged is the multi-dimensional "mirror" of our Triune-God in Christ. To understand this mirror, we must remember how mankind was first created: "Then God [*Father, Son, Spirit*] said, 'Let **Us** [*three Coequals*] make man in **Our image** [*a created 'us' in relational coequality*] according to **Our likeness** [*sacrificial Self-sharers in fusion oneness*]…'" (Gen. 1:26). When we human beings fell into "**the lie**" (John 8:44; Rom. 3:7) of eros individualism and self-worth-ship, we were no longer the **mirror image** of the "Us" who created us. Therefore, for the truth of our Triune-Creator to be revealed to us and in us, it was necessary that all three Eternals come in "fullness" both in the Son Jesus Christ, the Prototype Man, as well as in the Spirit of Christ, our Re-gene-rator. Paul explained:

But we all [*as coequal "members" of Christ*], with unveiled face [*the eclipse of individualism and self-focus removed*], beholding as in a **mirror** the glory of the Lord [*three Coequals in fusion in the Nucleus of Christ*], are being **transformed** [*lit. morphed*] **into the same image** from glory to glory [*a process of corporate maturity in fusion oneness*], just as from the Lord, the Spirit (2 Cor. 3:18).

Simply stated, it is not just me, but "we" together who must look into this mirror and be **corporately morphed** into the image and likeness of our Triune-Creator. Soren Kierkegaard wrote:

Admirers [*as contrasted with true followers*]... refuse to accept that **Christ's life is a demand** [*the requirement of the law of Triune-Agape*]. In actual fact, they are offended by Him [*His infinite worth is an affront to self-worth-ship*]. His radical, bizarre character [*sacrificially upholding the coequality of people whom they consider inferior and unworthy*] so often offends them that when they honestly see Christ for who He is [*the God-Man Nucleus and Equalizer*], they are no longer able to experience the tranquility they so much seek after [*to remain undisturbed: a law unto themselves*].

They know full well that to associate with Him too closely [*incorporation into His corpus*] amounts to being **up for examination** [*the God-Man is "a two-edged sword piercing as far as the division of soul and spirit...able to judge the thoughts and intentions of the heart" Heb. 4:12*]. Even though **He says nothing against them personally** [*"If anyone hears My sayings and does not keep them, I do not judge him..." John 5:22*], they know that **His life tacitly judges theirs** (Soren Kierkegaard, "Followers, Not Admirers," from *Provocations: Spiritual Writings of Kierkegaard*, Orbis, 2003).

Jesus described the nature of this verdict of judgment, which we as His fellow human beings will face both individually and corporately, through the "mirror" image and likeness of our Triune-Creator:

Will God not bring about justice for His elect [*whom the Spirit has incorporated into My many-membered corpus*] **who cry to Him day and night** [*e.g. proactive sons and daughters waiting expectantly for "the God of justice" rather than reacting with man-made justice?*], **and will He delay long over them? I tell you that He** [*"a consuming fire, a jealous God" Deut. 4:24*] **will bring about justice for them quickly. However, when the Son of Man comes** [*as the Equalizer and Judge in* *unshielded Light: the God-Man Nucleus of the fusion of the Trinity and man]* **will He find faith** *[faith-full sacrificial self-sharers fused together in coequality—"imitators of God as beloved children"—a Trinity-like 'us']* **on the earth?**" (Luke 18:7-8).

In the next volume, *God Magnified Part 12: Embracing the Consuming Fire*, we will magnify the following, related *God is* statements:

For the Lord, whose name is **Jealous**, is a jealous God *[three Eternals jealous-for One Another and jealous-for us]* (Ex. 34:14).

For the Lord your God is a **consuming fire** *[a fusion Vortex]*, a jealous God (Deut. 4:24).

For **love** *[Triune-Agape]* is as strong as death, **jealousy** *[jealousy-for]* is as severe as Sheol; its flashes are **flashes of fire** *[e.g. "God is a sun" Ps. 84:11]*, the very **flame of the Lord** *[e.g. Holy, Holy, Holy in perpetual fusion]* (Songs 8:6).

Therefore, since we *[coequal "members" of Christ]* receive a **kingdom** *[cohabitation of the Trinity and man in fusion in the Nucleus of a God-Man]* which cannot be shaken *[un-fission-able]*, let us show gratitude *[reciprocal gene-rosity]*, by which we may offer to God an acceptable service [*as one, new, many-membered, Self-sharing Man in Christ*] with reverence and awe; for our God is a **consuming fire** (Heb. 12:28-29).

P.O. Box 3709 ❖ Cookeville, TN 38502
931.520.3730 ❖ lc@lifechangers.org

CPSIA information can be obtained at www.ICGtesting.com
Printed in the USA
LVOW10s0950080616

491510LV00003B/3/P

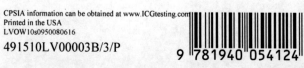